PRAISE FOR
HARD TO KEEP HAPPY

"Adam hits all of life's events at a basic level and gives his personal twist and advice. He uses quotes that tie into his stories and injects humor and personal experiences within the material. A great read!!"

—Kevin Beaulieu, Major, USAF (Ret.)

"Flight engineers have the challenge of keeping an multimillion-dollar aircraft flying, in spite of the pilots. A first sergeant is the leader of the enlisted force and the commander's go-to for advice. As a father, flight engineer, and first sergeant with the special operations community, Adam Thompson is one of the finest men I have ever served beside. He has captured some very hard-won lessons about living, loving, and finding satisfaction in our lives. This book should be a must-read for the young college student, military member, and the up-and-coming business person. You don't just make it happen; you have to work your ass off to make it happen. Happiness is a choice we all have to make. This book is a road map."

—Frank Dailey, Chief Master Sergeant, USAF (Ret.)

"This is a must-read! Adam delivers an insightful pathway to maintaining joy. We all face challenging times; however, Adam equips the reader with the tools needed to overcome the challenges and struggles of life. Simply put, this book will assist you in maintaining a joyful life!"

—Michael Von Ahnen, Chief Master Sergeant, USAF (Ret.)

Hard to Keep Happy: How to Maintain Lasting Joy in Challenging Times
by Adam J. Thompson

© Copyright 2024 Adam J. Thompson

ISBN 979-8-88824-189-9

All rights reserved. No part of this publication may be reproduced, stored in a retrieval system, or transmitted in any form or by any means—electronic, mechanical, photocopy, recording, or any other—except for brief quotations in printed reviews, without the prior written permission of the author.

Published by

3705 Shore Drive
Virginia Beach, VA 23455
800-435-4811
www.koehlerbooks.com

HARD TO KEEP HAPPY

How to Maintain Lasting Joy in Challenging Times

HARD TO KEEP HAPPY

How to Maintain Lasting Joy in Challenging Times

ADAM J. THOMPSON

VIRGINIA BEACH
CAPE CHARLES

CONTENTS

Introduction 1

SECTION I—Health 17
Chapter 1: Happiness Requires Health 19
Chapter 2: Happiness Requires Discipline 23
Chapter 3: Happiness Requires Learning 35
Chapter 4: Happiness Requires Temperance 52
Chapter 5: Happiness Requires Struggle 69

SECTION II—Wealth 23
Chapter 6: Gross Domestic Prosperity 93

SECTION III—Love 113
Chapter 7: Relationships and Happiness 115
Chapter 8: Pleasure and Happiness 130
Chapter 9: Love and Happiness 152

Afterword 166
Acknowledgments 169
Notes 170

INTRODUCTION

Do you want to live a happier, flourishing, more satisfying life with far less stress? Shouldn't we all? Do you want to share that happiness with your family, friends, coworkers, and other humans? Of course you do! Well, valued customer, step right up and let me show you how I can help you live that happier, fuller, more satisfying life.

HARD TO KEEP HAPPY

The story starts in a small Thai restaurant in Mary Esther, Florida. The one with the best Pad Thai in town, by the way. It was there while having lunch with a good friend and, like many of our lunchtime conversations, we discussed our journeys through personal growth. I just want to throw out that if you don't have these types of conversations with close friends, I recommend you start. They're amazing, therapeutic, and not only help you become a better person, but I will also argue that they help you become closer friends. Just a suggestion. But I digress. We were having one of those personal growth conversations, and it was my turn to share. We had talked about the last three years of my life, facing the loss of close friends and loved ones, changes in my Air Force career, and just overall living. The kids were growing up too fast, as kids tend to do, and I was doing my best to juggle being a husband, a father, and a career military man. All the good things, the bad things, what made things better, and what made things worse. After I was done, my friend took a deep breath, looked me square in the eye, and, after stealing a couple of tasty noodles from my plate, said, "You are hard to keep happy."

I will admit that my colleague's comment did not surprise me at all. There was no grand epiphany, no angels singing, not even a cartoon lightbulb going off above my head. My comrade was correct. I *am* hard to keep happy, and I bet you are, too.

My compatriot continued to describe me as this flower that, while wanting constant watering, didn't necessarily *need* to be watered every day. Guess that makes me a cactus. That's okay; cacti are cool. That's why every tourist who comes to Florida wants to buy one instead of a palm or other native Gulf Coast plant . . . you know, instead of going to someplace more appropriate like Arizona. However, even the resilient cactus needs to be hydrated from time to time, or it will eventually die. So, when I don't get the proverbial water, I feel my happiness level decline. Now, that seems like a straightforward solution, right? We have basic needs that, if not fulfilled, put us in a negative state of being. It doesn't take a rocket scientist to figure that out. But I had some questions to answer.

Why was I waiting for it to rain instead of finding a puddle? Why was I waiting for someone else to water me when I should be finding the water myself? Why was I waiting for someone else to make me happy when I should be trying to keep myself happy continuously?

I have no reason to be unhappy, mind you. I am very blessed in my life. I am blessed with an amazing spouse who is extremely supportive and loving; we have two awesome kids who we have watched grow into young adults; we own a nice house in a quiet neighborhood; and we both have successful careers we are content with. So, what the hell is my problem? Maybe you're like me and are asking the same thing.

It's not entirely anyone's fault because, in the modern world, your senses are constantly bombarded with multiple stimuli telling you that you need the next new cell phone and the next gas-guzzling car or the new electric, self-driving car. Won't that be nice? Or you need the bigger home with the hot tub and she-shed in the backyard in the most modern of neighborhoods, with the most annoying homeowner's association, too. You are never given time to sit and just *be*. And you need to just be in the moment and enjoy what you have.

Don't get me wrong, material things are nice, but they are not the cause of our sorrows. It's just that they alone cannot be the proverbial mortar to fill the gaps in our emotional brick walls. Don't believe me? Go find any celebrity out there. Millions of dollars in the bank, a fifty-room mansion, a fleet of cars, and all the perks, yet they've been divorced two or three times, have had mental breakdowns on national television, or just have slipped into the hell that is depression and loneliness. The money didn't make them sad; not finding the things that truly make them happy makes them sad.

> "Happiness begins with the decision to no longer feel sad."
> —Steven Aitchison

I had a very successful military career, spending two decades in the US Air Force, and I will tell you that from the beginning of that career, the mentality was always, "What's the next thing?" The next promotion, the next duty station, the next deployment, the next opportunity. The military takes type-A personalities and makes them the most hungry, ambitious creatures on the planet. There's a need for those personalities in the realm of national defense, so that ambition is not necessarily a bad thing. I would like to point out that most things in life are neither good nor bad. Good and bad are values *we* place on things to manage our perceptions and expectations. I found, however, that always looking to the next thing didn't give me much time to appreciate where I was and what I was doing *at that moment*. It took me nearly eighteen years in uniform to finally figure out I needed to just *be* and find contentment right where I already was.

So, if I had all that I needed to be happy—a distinguished career, an amazing family, a big house, etc.—then why the hell was I unhappy? And even more so, why am I hard to *keep* happy?

The word *keep* means two things: to retain or to support a continued condition. The first refers to getting something, in this case, *happiness,* and the second refers to maintaining the continued state of that happiness. I can get happiness and not just from material things. I find happiness in my relationships, in my career opportunities, in reading a good book while sitting on the patio with a cup of coffee, or in drinking a cold beer watching the New England Patriots play football. It's maintaining that sense of happiness that I struggle with. Let me emphasize that I used the word *struggle* and not *struggled* because it is a constant battle within the human condition to be happy. Like anything good, it takes time, discipline, and commitment to its mastery.

I think you find yourself there, too. We all do. It's not some rare instance that only a few suffer through. As I said, it is the human condition, and we all live it every day to some degree.

It's normal. Congratulations, you're human.

That doesn't mean we can't get better or grow or develop as we go. Then we can take those lessons learned and help others through their journey to find happiness in this madhouse called life. We're all in this together, right?

WHY I WROTE THIS BOOK

I wrote this book because the best way to figure out how to improve on how to be happy is by helping others who are on the same journey as you. And therapy is just too damn expensive. If you're going to be a happier person, then you need to break down things a little. Get your hands—and your minds—a little dirty as you dig up some truth. There are a million books, videos, and seminars out there that try to tell you how to find and live "the good life." What the hell does that even *mean*? Do I have to be wealthy to live the good life? Doesn't hurt, I guess. Does it mean having beautiful women or handsome men on our arms, partying it up on Las Vegas Boulevard? Sounds fun until you get too old to take a hangover. Is it the mansion on the California coast or Martha's Vineyard? Maybe, if you need ten thousand square feet with a ten-car garage and three swimming pools, you could live in for twenty years and never see the entire residence to make you smile.

If all of those are your things, then great! Who the hell am I to judge? Or anyone, for that matter. I would argue, however, that there are plenty of unhappy rich people in this world, a plethora of individuals who still feel lonely, even in a crowd. Those big houses leave a lot of room for emptiness. I am not bashing those things. Those lives can be the culmination of years of hard work and turmoil to reach a high level of success. But, as I have stated—in case you weren't paying attention the first time—*things* don't make us happy. So, what does?

I would further contend that there are simpler, more cost-effective ways for you to live the good life. To be happy. *Genuine happiness* is the deep state of an individual's being that leads to an almost full sense of being content with life, in which one can bravely face what life has in store every day. It's the kind of contentment where you can find joy living in a three-hundred-square-foot closet in New York City or a ten-acre farm in northern Maine. This contentment creates resiliency that allows an individual to bounce back from adversity and, further, to be a source of strength for others. It is the kind of joy that comes from a robust sense of purpose, a life lived with excellence, and a life lived with an enduring sense of duty.

Sound hokey? Maybe it is, maybe it isn't. That's really for you to decide on your own. Reread that last paragraph again. Dissect its words. It is the *deep state* of an individual's *being*. A sense of being is a sign we are living evolved lives, at peace with ourselves, our environment, and even our past. It means to be content in your future, wherever that may lead. The statement goes further to talk about being content but doing so bravely in the face of adversity. This is resiliency and a strong sense of core beliefs coupled with those things that make you mentally, physically, emotionally, and spiritually stronger. It's the whole *When life gives you lemons, make lemonade* mentality . . . only then you add some vodka to that bad boy! Being a source of strength to others is vitally important here because humans are social creatures. We need each other, and we need healthy relationships to find fulfillment in life. To be happy, to be content, and to be resilient means being positively affecting others. Remember the adage, "It's better to give than to receive." There is some science to that.

To live a life with excellence and an enduring sense of duty means to live up to great potential. Keep learning. Read the books. Hell, you're reading this one now, aren't you? Find ways to improve yourself and others. What do you feel a sense of duty toward? Is it God, country, king, family, your career, or the Boston Red Sox? Okay, okay, maybe not the Red Sox. But you should find what inspires you to be dutiful and make yourself an example of that.

In helping others, you'll find a high sense of purpose that will lead to increased happiness. I mean, hell, it's science! Understand that true happiness is not something that can be purchased, subscribed to, chartered, borrowed, or even pilfered. It must be self-generated continuously, daily, consistently, and in a way that fits one's character. If done right, it will withstand all of life's hardships and misfortunes and be a fortress of satisfaction and serenity. But before we can start this epic journey to discovering *true happiness,* we must first examine what *true happiness* means.

> "Happiness is either where you are now, or it is nowhere at all."
>
> —Buddha (maybe . . . probably)

You don't think about wanting to be happy until the day comes when you truly realize you just aren't happy any longer. It comes right out of the blue and sucker punches you like some barroom brawler when you looked at his biker girlfriend the wrong way—the proverbial beer-bottle-over-the-head moment that leaves you bleeding, bruised, and smelling of cheap, shitty beer—and you come to the realization "Holy hell, what happened? I'm not happy anymore." The good news, though, is that everyone seems to have the answer to your problem.

Drink this drink, drive this car, wear these clothes, sleep with these people, and you, too, can be the hap-hap-happiest asshole on this side of the nuthouse. Not happy with your looks? You can get Botox and collagen and wear some makeup sponsored by this big-bosomed actress. Wear your hair like this pop star. Wear the same sneakers as this superstar athlete. Not happy with your weight? For thirty minutes a day, twenty minutes a day, eight minutes a day, just six minutes a day, and you can lose weight and look great in a speedo!

C'mon, folks, really? What the hell?

Maybe you *will* be happy . . . until the Botox wears off, or the makeup runs or someone more famous releases their own brand of sneaker that's more popular than the ones you bought—but then you're unhappy again. The six-minute workouts might save you time and energy and make you think you're getting results, but until you come to a level of satisfaction and comfort with your body, you can do sit-ups until you puke, and it won't make a damn bit of a difference. Are you still not convinced? That's fair. Let's keep digging deeper, then.

Maybe you hate your job because you no longer find value in the work or with the company. It could be a troubled relationship with a spouse, partner, or lover because you cannot communicate or connect anymore. Ever sit at your desk late after work just for the simple reason that you don't want to go home and face the person who's in your house? It could just be that your favorite football team didn't make it to the playoffs this season . . . again. Maybe you think you'll find happiness at the bottom of a bottle-of-bourbon well. I tried that, too, and it didn't work.

But whatever the crux, I have some good news: there is a way.

After all these pages, are you asking, "What the hell does being happy *really* mean? When are you going to get to the punchline?" Well, here's the thing: to be happy is so subjective. To one person, happiness means having a lot of money but, of course, how much is enough? To others, it is having a big family, a good job, or a successful career. But what are the matrices for that level of happiness? To some, being happy just means the ability to sit on the couch and watch football with a cold beer without having to get up and take out the trash. Pass the Sam Adams and go Pats!

Author Tom Bodett, the guy who used to advertise for Motel 6 ("I'm Tom Bodett for Motel 6, and we'll leave the lights on for you"), also said, and more importantly, "A person needs just three things to be truly happy in this world: someone to love, something to do, and something to hope for." Stoic philosophy, in general, tends to agree with Tom's sentiment. For thousands of years philosophers, theologians, psychologists, and every self-proclaimed messiah in between have tried to seek understanding in the abstract and subjective concept that lies in the query *How can I be happy?*

Let's take a minute to break down happiness into its basic protons and neutrons. Webster's Dictionary defines happiness as 1) the state of being happy (well, duh); 2) good fortune, pleasure, contentment, or joy. Nataly Kogan, CEO of the learning platform *Happier*, and author of the book *Happier Now: How to Stop Chasing Perfection and Embrace Everyday Moments (Even the Difficult Ones)*, says that happiness "isn't something you feel. It's something you do." Therefore, happiness requires action and activity. I'm pretty sure I told you that already. Happiness is not a personality trait; it is a state of mind or what psychologists call *subjective well-being*. It is a finite status that is fleeting, changeable, and even negotiable. We must find the things in life that put us in a state of being content, and those things vary from person to person.

Another question is how do we make happiness consistent? Well, frankly, it's impossible unless you're constantly taking some good drugs, and even then, the crash is inevitable. We must understand and accept that we cannot be happy 100 percent of the time. It's entirely impossible, so don't try! What we can do is strive to push through those unhappy times to find a balanced level of stability in our lives as we pursue this higher meaning of happiness I keep rambling about. Well, you've read this far; how about you go a little farther?

A NEWFOUND PHILOSOPHY

> "Imagine smiling after a slap in the face. Then think of doing it twenty-four hours a day."
> —Markus Zusak

I had a rough couple of years from 2018–2020. I'll tell some stories in the coming chapters, but I'll start by sharing a philosophy I found during this time called Stoicism. Developed in Athens, Greece, in the third century BCE, Stoicism is a philosophy that teaches that living virtuously is the highest *good*, based on the continued quest for knowledge and the decision to live in harmony with nature, all while accepting that reason and logic govern nature. It is a practical philosophy, meaning that it must be practiced. The words themselves help inspire and motivate but are meaningless without action. That's what I found so intriguing about it. You can't just sit on your ass and read some anecdotes to find happiness. There are plenty of fools out there who think that's the way. But it's not.

However, as excited as I was about my newfound philosophy, I struggled to find the support I wanted from my peers. When you start using terms like *Greco-Roman philosophy* and names like *Seneca, Epictetus, Rufus,* and *Marcus Aurelius,* you tend to lose people who don't want to see what those terms and those names stand for. To them, they're hokey. I might as well have been practicing voodoo and keeping a pet Raven in my office. They would smile and nod when I told them about the concepts but tuned me out as if I were trying to sell them used Tupperware warped in the dishwasher. I'll admit it became a bit defeating, so I started keeping those interests to myself. This is a huge shame because one of the tenets of Stoicism is our ability to coexist and make other human beings better with our search for wisdom. Nevertheless, I kept going.

Stoic philosophy is simple. Happiness is a *journey*, not a destination. If you wait to die happy, then you will never really live. Throughout this journey, you're supposed to live virtuously. Become a wiser person, a more courageous person, someone who lives moderately and always seeks to care for others as individuals, groups, and even mankind. Last, you do this by only truly caring about what you have absolute control over. Absolute control means dedicating precious energy to and not being sidetracked by things you cannot influence. That piece is hard, but when you realize what few things you have *absolute* control over, you realize you don't have as much control as you think.

Seriously, when that part sinks in, and I mean *really* sinks in, there's a moment of terror before the sense of peace sets in.

So, why worry needlessly and waste energy and resources on things you cannot affect? I did not want to write a book about Stoic philosophy, however. There are plenty of authors more qualified to do that. But what I'm going to tell you is, based on this level of thinking, and more importantly, the idea that action is required.

I'LL HAVE THE EUDEMONIA WITH A SIDE OF TZATZIKI, PLEASE.

The ancient Greek and Roman philosophers, both the Stoics and those who inspired the Stoics, had fundamental ideas on happiness they expressed in a term called *eudaemonia*. It's a funny Greek word that has little to do with spit-roasted lamb splattered in yummy yogurt sauce. Loosely translated, eudaemonia means "to be happy." It has a much deeper, more significant connotation, however. Eudemonia means "to thrive" or "to flourish." The ancient Greek thinkers believed that human flourishing and prosperity are ongoing activities from which happiness stems. If happiness has strata, then eudaemonia is the utmost zenith. It is more than being content with things or people or your environment. It is a deep level of contentment with your current financial status, your current relationships, your job, your dog, the color of your drapes, and your life in general.

The Greek philosopher Socrates, the father of Western philosophy and modern thinking, believed that eudaemonia was the highest goal of all mankind. He expressed it was a divine gift to the world, given from a higher power, but because of its holiness, this level of happiness was inaccessible to humans. Nevertheless, despite being a lofty goal, Socrates felt that man should strive for it anyway, that we must endeavor to attain the unattainable. He further induced that one should live virtuously to reach that higher state of happiness.

Socrates's pupil, Plato, brought the concept of eudaemonia down a few levels to something more within humanity's reach. Plato believed happiness was achievable, but because of man's gravitational pull to vice, the proverbial ground to be covered in the quest for eudaemonia becomes a spiritual battlefield in each person's soul. Vices are those things considered being immoral or at least unhealthy, such as gambling, excessive drinking, and snorting cocaine off a hooker. Okay, you get the point—things that are fun at the time but eventually become counterproductive and detract from the longevity of the human condition. In Plato's view, to beat vice and achieve happiness, a person must live virtuously, and even then, it is a struggle because vices provide fleeting pleasures.

Plato illustrates his point in the second book of his writing, the *Republic*. He tells the tale of the magical Ring of Gyges, a mythical artifact that makes its wearer invisible. A shepherd in the Ionian kingdom of Lydia finds this magical ring and uses it to seduce the queen. The shepherd convinces the queen to assassinate her husband, the king, and establish the shepherd as ruler. It's reads like something straight out of Jerry Springer . . . with a mythical twist.

Plato theorized in this tale that if a just man had no fear of the consequences of his negative actions, then he would be tempted to act unjustly all the time. He emphasizes eudaemonia can only be achieved with a heavy attentiveness to justice. The parable demonstrates how murdering a dignitary to take power and shacking up with someone else's wife is counterproductive to virtuous living and being happy over the long term.

This brings us to Aristotle. If Plato is the ancient Greek Obi-Wan Kenobi, then Aristotle is very much the Luke Skywalker of the era, minus Darth Vader and a galactic space war, of course. Plato's pupil proceeds to pontificate the perception of ultimate happiness a little further but a bit more grounded. Aristotle agreed with his tutor that eudaemonia was achievable through virtuous living but argued that it is not enough just to *be* virtuous; a person had to *live* virtuously.

Remember, happiness requires action and activity. See the theme here?

We have to get off our asses occasionally, and wise old Aristotle agreed with this. You cannot just *be* wise; you must seek out wisdom and knowledge. You cannot just *be* courageous; you must act courageously. It is not enough to *be* temperate but must live in moderation. It is not enough to believe in justice; you must be a just person in thought and action. Marcus Aurelius, one of the most benevolent and wisest of the Roman emperors, stated, "The impediment to action advances action. What stands in the way becomes the way." Marcus Aurelius is talking about how to deal with the obstacles in our lives with this quote. However, to make a proper point, if *inaction is* keeping you from being happy, then *action* will overcome that obstacle.

HAPPINESS LEADS TO SUCCESS

> "It is neither wealth nor splendor; but tranquility and occupation which give you happiness."
> —Thomas Jefferson

There have been nearly two hundred studies on happiness conducted on over a quarter of a million people worldwide for years, and the results all lean in the same direction: happiness leads to success. More importantly, *your* happiness leads to *your* success. My happiness cannot be your happiness. Your success cannot be my success. It must be unique to our situation, our values, our passions, and our desires. However, you must ask yourself, what is your definition of success? If happiness leads to success, then what does that look like? Success is a form of achievement, the end goal. Remember that happiness is not found at the destination; it is found on the journey. Success is a milestone on that journey. It is the island you conquered that will be the jumping-off point for a new mission. It is the end of one chapter as the next one is being written. Whatever analogy or metaphor you need to make the puzzle complete in your mind, use it.

The difference in this discussion is that success can be seen from the outside by other people. Happiness is not always the case. People will judge your success based on their values and their personal definitions of success. Can you be successful and not happy? Absolutely. I would argue, however, that if you're happy, *truly happy*, flourishing, thriving, and prospering, that, my friend, is success in and of itself.

A CALL TO ACTION

> "The universe calls you to action with a good swift kick to the shins. It hurts, but it gets the job done."
>
> —Aaron Polson

Here is my bottom line for all of this: happiness requires three main components—health, wealth, and love. There is a surplus of subtopics. We'll discuss what those three things are and what they mean to you. Regardless of where your launchpad is, remember this: happiness starts with you. Just *you*. Not your relationships, not your job, not your money, not your porcelain Marylin Monroe cookie jar. You. So, if you're not happy right now, what do you plan on doing about it? What is your call to action?

I wrote this book to show you that while mankind's search for happiness has been long and enduring, it is absolutely achievable for everyone. Happiness means something different for everyone, but these are the three main elements we all need in our sojourn to satisfaction. All three of these, health, wealth, and love, require action on our part. But before we can act, we need to be educated. Let me be your tutor, your Plato, your spirit guide. Let me help you on your journey to find your happiness.

FRIENDLY WARNING

Before we begin, I want to start with a friendly warning. Yup, a warning. This is a self-help book. Self-help books often get a lot of shade thrown their way because some people see the term *self-help* as an oxymoron, if not a fallacy. There are those who come right out and say that it doesn't work. Well, that depends on the reader. This isn't a medical textbook on how to *fix* your life. On the contrary, this is a roadmap, a book of tactics and techniques, a personal view from my own life experiences that you may use or not use as you see fit to find your positive outcome. As I mentioned before, humans have been seeking the path to happiness for thousands of years. And we have tried finding it any way we can, whether through religion, philosophy, astrology, books, or in bottles and empty relationships. If mankind had figured it out already, there wouldn't be any need for any of these things, including this book. So, we keep struggling, and thinking, and writing those thoughts down in hopes of making our lives better.

I'm not offering a *fix*. Happiness isn't a "one and done." If I take a painkiller, the headache goes away, right? No! The painkiller only hides the true cause of why you have a headache in the first place. A theme you will see throughout this book is *action*. Happiness requires you to do something, much like reading this book. I don't offer a fix; I offer strategies, a new perception, or at least a different consideration of the subject at hand. For example, sometimes being happy means to *stop* doing something. Stopping doing something or doing nothing at all can be a challenge in and of itself. This is a book about personal growth—my personal growth—which I have translated to text in hopes of fueling your personal growth. I want you to think about what it means for you to be happy and how you can achieve small victories in your life that you can pass on to others and help them discover strategies that will, in turn, give them small victories in their lives.

> "The key to all happiness is not to try and make everyone happy."
>
> —Socrates

SECTION I

HEALTH

CHAPTER 1
HAPPINESS REQUIRES HEALTH

> *The groundwork of all happiness is good health.*
>
> **—Leigh Hunt**

Pretend for a moment that I have a time machine. It's not much to look at—lots of duct tape and bubble gum hold it together. For the sake of argument, this time machine works and gives us the ability to travel back through the annals of history. We're going way back, back to the earliest days of primitive man. Back to a time when humans were short, hairy, sparsely clothed in animal skins, and living in caves. These early humans were omnivores, eating fruits they could pick, root vegetables they could dig up, and scavenging meat from animals left behind by larger carnivorous creatures who left scraps after eating their fill. They ate their food raw, and our furry, smelly friends here have not discovered, let alone mastered, the control of fire and, subsequently, the art of cooking. Their brains were much smaller than ours, and verbal language was still primitive. It will take a few thousand years, but man will eventually master the control of fire so they can keep warm, fight off predatory animals, and cook food.

Studies have found a correlation between brain size and eating meat and the consequent brain growth from eating cooked foods.

The consumption of larger amounts of proteins aided in the growth of human intelligence. Also, the act of cooking makes food easier to chew and digest, allowing more nutrients to be extracted and, thus, more energy to be absorbed. Steak made us smarter. That's what I'm trying to sell you here. I love steak.

All right, let's get back in our jalopy of a time machine. As our time-travel journey moves forward, we see our ancestors learning how to hunt and trap both small game, like wild goats and pigs, and then larger animals, like bears and woolly mammoths. This is providing more protein and enables the continued growth of the human brain. However, hunting and gathering are not enough to maintain large populations.

Sometime around 10,000 BCE, farming begins in the Fertile Crescent and spreads throughout the rest of the Middle East, Africa, and Asia. A couple of thousand years later, we see our innovative ancestors domesticate animals like cows, sheep, and pigs to be used for milk and meat. This allows the required dietary requirements to grow the human population into larger areas. And while man won't start learning about nutrition as a science until 400 BCE, it can easily be ascertained how these early humans know that they needed to eat and that some things were better to eat than others.

Let's jump ahead again. (Bill and Ted should have come with us.) We can see the same foundation to understand exercise in Greece circa 600 BCE. The Greeks are comprehending how physical exercise can increase a person's strength, speed, and endurance. Even bodybuilding is being developed to enhance the human physique. But it's not until our time machine reaches the twentieth century that we will see our modern selves grasp both nutrition and fitness to enhance health and increase longevity. Now, as we step out of our time machine, welcome back to the twenty-first century. I want to show you that health, wellness, and physical activity can lead us to a better state of well-being and a higher form of happiness.

> "Believe you can and you're halfway there."
> —Theodore Roosevelt

Our little time-travel trip was quick, I admit, but it is easy to see that the ancestors we observed lived a life of difficulty. Little in life comes easy; happiness is not excluded. Yet there, unlike our cavemen forebears, some people still will not put in the necessary effort to get the value-added rewards of hard work. Understand that the goal is to find ways to make our lives more content, a life that is flourishing, thriving, and prospering. In other words, a happy life. Happiness is not a lack of work, nor is it the lack of negative emotions. Happiness does involve reducing negative emotions like shame, anger, guilt, self-doubt, self-loathing, negative stress, etc. All the icky feelings that keep us . . . well . . . unhappy. Self-discipline can help with this.

Self-discipline is the ability of a person to get past those negative feelings and make the choices that invoke positive results. It comes with some prerequisites, however, such as the ability to think critically, problem-solve, cultivate healthy relationships, and ultimately make positive choices that lead to constructive outcomes.

> "Life doesn't get easier or more forgiving, we get stronger and more resilient."
> — Steve Maraboli

Struggle is a necessary inconvenience in life. There is a grave misconception that happiness is a state without any kind of inconvenience, embarrassment, friction, or any bad things happening to us in general. That's just not fundamentally true. The truth is, if you did live such a life—one without any inconvenience or trouble—

then you would only be living a life in a bubble, sheltered and naive to the harsh realities of living.

In Mark Manson's best-selling book, *The Subtle Art of Not Giving a F*ck,* he writes that "The avoidance of struggle *is* a struggle. The denial of failure *is* a failure. Hiding what is shameful *is* itself a form of shame." What Manson is getting at is that in life, we must experience pain and embarrassment and all those things that suck in life in order to have a good life. I get it; it seems like a paradox. Manson calls it a *mind-fuck* in his book, but when it sinks in, then it all makes perfect sense. Everyone likes to use the caterpillar becoming a butterfly analogy to show a change in life because it is an extreme change, going from a creepy crawly wormy thing to becoming an elegant, flying organism that everyone adores. No female college freshman gets a tattoo of a caterpillar on their ankle—it is always a butterfly. However, what many people don't know is that the struggle inside the pupa of the caterpillar becoming a butterfly is integral to the process. If you try to cut the pupa, thinking you are helping release the butterfly from its organic prison, the butterfly, regardless of the stage of change, will die. This is because that struggle is essential to the metamorphosis and the butterfly's very survival.

> "Self-control is strength. Right thought is mastery. Calmness is power."
>
> **—James Allen**

One way to be happy is to understand that you don't control as much as you think you do. And the sooner you grasp this concept and further accept that you should only focus on what you do control, life gets a little easier.

CHAPTER 2
HAPPINESS REQUIRES DISCIPLINE

> *Discipline is the path to happiness.*
> —Matthew Kelly

I hate running. Absolutely frigging hate it. In fact, those who run for "fun" are an utter astonishment to me. Even after serving two decades in the military, I still wonder why the hell someone would do that to their back and knees. All dramatics aside, and despite my loathing of the terrible trot, I recognize and acknowledge the benefits of running and of exercise in general. Truth be told, the most successful people in the world are avid exercisers, so there must be something to it. I know I need physical activity throughout my week to mentally recenter and physically find my balance. This all provides the ingredients of longevity for my overall health. It should go without saying that for us to be happy, we must be healthy. Now, truth be told, sitting on the couch eating cheesy poofs with your kitty while binge-watching all twenty-two seasons of your favorite show could make you content. However, over time that might not be the case. I'm also not advocating for you to become a gym rat if that's not your thing. I am by no means an image of Adonis, but I'm not a couch potato either.

> "I believe that the Good Lord gave us a finite number of heartbeats and I'm damned if I'm going to use up mine running up and down a street."
>
> —Neil Armstrong

One of Neil Armstrong's lesser-known quotes was, "I believe that the Good Lord gave us a finite number of heartbeats and I'm damned if I'm going to use up mine running up and down a street." I share in his logic, although the US military feels a little different from the first man to walk on the moon. Nevertheless, I capitulate to the fact that science has already found running, as well as all other forms of physical exercise, beneficial to our health and happiness.

In our modern, drive-through, one-click world, you are constantly bombarded with images of how your workout routines and diet plans are unequivocally inadequate. Every time you pull up an internet video, there is some ad with a sculpted, shirtless twenty-something-year-old-dude and enough hair product on his scalp to power a diesel engine, telling you that your workout routine, your diet, and your very existence sucks. Have no fear, however, if you listen to said sculpted, oily-headed dude, you can get the beach body you want in just a couple of weeks—for $49.99 a month, of course. Want to lose weight? Stop eating carbs, only eat kale, stand on one leg while drinking room temperature water and thinking happy thoughts, and you, too, can drop five, ten, or fifteen pounds in just a few days. C'mon. Really?

Maybe throw in some howling at the moon while dancing barefoot in the grass to better your chances of improving your chakras. By the way, kudos to those who have success with keto and other extremely low-carb diets. Living off twenty grams or fewer carbs a day is an absolute pain in the ass. Everything good to eat has carbs in it. I salute you! Dieting can work, but, like early retirement or those six-pack abs, it requires self-discipline.

DIET AND EXERCISE

> "No citizen has the right to be an amateur in the matter of physical training...What a disgrace it is for man to grow old without ever seeing the beauty and strength of which his body is capable."
>
> —Socrates

I spent most of my military career in Air Force Special Operations Command (AFSOC), the air arm of the United States Special Operations Command (USSOCOM). After years of fighting wars, mainly in the Middle East, USSOCOM began investing a lot of time, energy, and money into improving the overall health and welfare of our warfighters. Running ten miles with a hundred-pound rucksack and knocking out two hundred push-ups a day will keep you in shape but most definitely leads to chronic back pain in your late thirties. As you get older, more is required when recovering from a variety of injuries. USSOCOM developed a program called the Preservation of the Force and Family (POTFF), whose mission is to see to the physical, cognitive, psychological, and spiritual needs of both military members and their families. It is an amazing program, run by some awesome people, for the purpose of getting the servicemember back into the fight faster, building a resilient force, and providing better support for the military family. I am a product of the outstanding work of those people that make up this program. POTFF is primarily made up of psychologists, social workers, nutritionists and dietitians, physical therapists, strength coaches, athletic trainers, and nurses as case managers. They are all committed to the selfless work of helping our military members and their families through some of the darkest moments of their recovery processes.

The old jokes about alcoholism and divorce running rampant in the US Armed Forces are not funny. In truth, it is a very real dilemma brought on by the rigors of military life and decades of constant deployments. High alcohol consumption of military personnel between the ages of seventeen and twenty-five, which is the demographic of a first-term enlisted servicemember (the most prevalent demographic in the US Armed Forces), went from 24 percent in 2001 to 30 percent by 2020. In 2020, 41 percent of marriages of US citizens under the age of thirty ended in divorce, and the US military made up an average of 3 percent of those divorces.

A military member is no good to the unit when their spouse just sent them a Dear John or Dear Jane letter while they're isolated in a forward operating base in the middle of nowhere because the said spouse has been cheating or just can no longer stand the physical and emotional separation. Add children into the mix, and it is a formula for some severe mental health issues. Further, injured members who could not get healthier fast enough are often medically separated—or medically retired if they are lucky—and forced back into the civilian world with little help in the difficult transition process. Hence, the POTFF program was birthed to do a better job of caring for our men and women in uniform.

I write all of this because I have had the absolute privilege of working with the men and women who work in the program. They have taught me invaluable knowledge over the years. And at the time of this writing, I am still married and not a slave to alcohol. Understanding how to form good habits in your diet and exercise provides for a happier life, and I want to pass those years of learning on to you.

EXERCISE AND THE PURSUIT OF HAPPINESS

> "Unless you puke, faint, or die, keep going!"
>
> —Jillian Michaels

The ancient Romans used to put gladiators and slaves into the arena for the sole purpose of fighting, and sometimes killing, each other for entertainment. Bloodsport, bread, and beverages were provided to pacify the populace of plebes. We look back, as civilized as we think we are, and are astonished at the brutality of our ancestors, yet we do the same thing in the modern era. I'm not talking about mixed martial arts, boxing, or even American football. I'm referring to reality television. People will tune in all over the world to watch these reality shows filled with drama to excess. And many who work on these shows have admitted that if there is no drama, then the producers, writers, and editors will make some or make it look like there is some. Much like our Roman forebears sitting in the amphitheaters, we sit around the television, gawking at their tragedy for our amusement. All to forget the miserable debacle our own lives have become. One such show really took the cake . . . so to speak.

The Biggest Loser was an American television show that ran seventeen seasons from 2004 to 2016. The premise was to take obese men and women and have them compete for up to thirty weeks for a substantial monetary prize. They were assigned celebrity trainers, along with an army of nutritionists and medical professionals off-screen. Every day they would work out, learn how to eat cleaner and healthier, and at the end of the week, they would have a weigh-in to determine the results of all that grueling work. The person with the smallest amount of weight loss was eliminated from the show. Here is where the proverbial gladiatorial combat began.

First, the competition was coed, and typically, men will lose weight faster than women, so the men immediately had an advantage. Then, in the first two weeks, the contestants would see dramatic weight loss as their toned, sculpted, vegan, celebrity personal trainers ran them through hours and hours of intense physical training, like drill sergeants whipping a platoon of fresh recruits into fighting shape. On week three, however, the weight loss would come to an abrupt halt as the contestants' weight loss would plateau due to metabolic changes. Instead of double-digit losses, it would be three, two, or even a single pound of weight lost. And, just like in the spectacles of ancient Rome, someone had to leave the arena.

> "At the end of the day, your health is your responsibility."
> —Jillian Michaels

I want you to think about this: money was the end goal of the *Biggest Loser* competition, a $250,000 prize for winning. However, if you are a morbidly obese human being struggling to change your lifestyle, and you have the very real opportunity to have that life changed with health and longevity regained by some of the best trainers in the world, then it is reasonable to argue that money probably becomes less important to you. *Guaranteed.* Now, add the fact you are leaving your family, your job, and everything you hold dear for weeks or months at a time if you stay in the competition that long while you are suffering through this process. No pain, no gain, or no loss in this case. The good news is that you're seeing your body changing for the better. The bad news is that every week you are put on a scale in front of millions of viewers to see how "less fat" you are, and some of these contestants would start at three to four hundred pounds! If you didn't lose more weight than anyone else, you were gone. Sent home with only a little knowledge prescribed for the sake of the viewing entertainment of those said millions. Throughout the show, you would also be "tempted." Eat a slice of pizza or a piece of cake to earn points during the weigh-in. Or eat the most calories during a minigame to negatively affect the other team. You should eat healthy so that you can get healthier and add days back to your life, but eat these three thousand calories, and it may help you gain footing in the competition.

Holy hell! Are you seeing any issues with any of this yet?

If you watched the show enough, you could see the utter anguish both in the eyes of the contestants and the trainers who were paid to partake in this Circus Maximus of human suffering. But it was also more than just mere entertainment. People have an internal gauge by which we measure ourselves against such entertainment train wrecks so we can feel better about our own lives. We aren't four hundred pounds and being paraded on national television for everyone to laugh and point at or even cheer on, so we must be doing something right. *Right*?

We know that being overweight has major medical and psychological consequences and that being a healthier weight is ideal for our longevity. If we feel good both physically and mentally about how we see ourselves, then we can truly find a measure of happiness, which is the goal here. Mind you, I said to be a *healthy* weight, not *skinny* or *thin*, or look like some oiled-up bodybuilder eating M&Ms behind the stage in a little banana hammock. I said *healthy* because healthy might not mean a size zero dress or a thirty-two-inch waist or anything of the sort. Be careful with that level of thinking because that opens a new can of psychological hell that does not lead to happiness at all. Instead, it leads to further self-loathing, unnecessary disappointment, and depression.

Danny Cahill, a *Biggest Loser* contestant and season eight winner, stood somewhat dazed under a shower of confetti as his family rushed the *Biggest Loser* stage. In thirty weeks, he lost an astonishing 239 pounds, having started the competition at 430 pounds, and walked out of the winner's circle at an amazing 191 pounds and $250,000 richer. At that point in *Biggest Loser* history, he had lost the most weight on the show. Danny began an immediate tour around the United States, showcasing his change on a variety of talk shows, but seven years later, Danny admitted he regained a hundred pounds despite all his efforts. This just highlights the struggle people have with obesity and how genetics can influence our lives despite all our hard work and efforts. However, Danny has since become a successful author and motivational speaker, helping others in their struggles with obesity and on their journeys to find healthier and happier lives.

Medical professionals were at odds with the outcome of the *Biggest Loser* competition. Despite being supervised by trainers and medical professionals, the contestants were averaging ten-pound losses a week, with some male contestants losing twenty to thirty pounds in the first week alone! Modern established medical guidelines for weight loss are set at one to two pounds a week for many years. Also, losing weight is only the first battle. Keeping the weight off has always been the bigger challenge for those struggling with obesity. Further, the contestants' diet consisted of severe caloric restriction, which comes with health hazards, such as weakening the cardiovascular system and dangerous vitamin deficiencies. Not a great addition to someone who may already have heart disease created by an unhealthy lifestyle. But, watching people eat right, work out a couple of hours a day, and only lose one or two pounds a week doesn't make good television for those plebians wanting to see action in the digital coliseum, but it does mean a healthy lifestyle for those of us who aren't reality television personalities.

The Centers for Disease Control and Prevention state that 90 percent of the United States' annual healthcare budget of $3.8 trillion (2021) is from patients with chronic health conditions such as those related to poor health and diet. Heart disease remains the number one killer of Americans (as of 2021). Some 868,000 Americans will die every year from heart disease or a stroke. That's a third of all deaths in the US annually! This stresses the US healthcare system and costs over $200 billion a year and, additionally, causes nearly $138 billion in economic damages from lost wages and productivity in the US labor force. My father died of a heart attack that was more than likely brought on by months of high blood pressure and other ailments he ignored for months before his passing. I loved my father, but he was stubborn. Diabetes affects another thirty-four million Americans, with an additional eighty-eight million at risk of Type II diabetes, which can cause heart disease, kidney failure, and blindness. In 2017, diabetes alone cost the US a total of $327 billion in healthcare costs and lost wages.

Not taking care of yourself will not only kill you but incur thousands, even millions, of dollars in costs to your family, your community, and our society at large. There is nothing happy about any of that for anyone. It doesn't matter if you're a couch potato or a gym rat; we all must pay attention to our health and wellness for a happier, more flourishing life. What choices will you make? What are you going to do about your current situation? Want to make it better? If so, keep reading.

NUTRITION AND THE PURSUIT OF HAPPINESS

What if I told you that you can lose weight by eating nothing but cream-filled chocolate sandwich cookies? You'd probably think I was full of it, right? Well, let me tell you a tale.

Once upon a time, there was a man named Mark Haub. Haub was a professor and the head of the Human Nutrition Department at Kansas State University. He became known as the Twinkie Guy because he claimed that he had lost approximately twenty-seven pounds in ten weeks by subsisting only on high-carbohydrate and sugary snacks such as Oreos, Doritos, Twinkies, and other such junk foods. Professor Twinkie, as I like to call him, asserted that he had accomplished this because his caloric intake was less than his caloric outtake—in other words, he was burning more calories than he was consuming. The theory here was that he was losing weight and therefore could eat anything he wanted. Many of the snack food companies, like Coca-Cola, jumped on this. As purveyors of sugary snacks, the idea of telling consumers they can lose weight and still partake in the junk food jamboree was more than just a gold mine of sales and marketing. It did get people thinking more about how the consumption of calories works.

There must be more to this story, right? You can't just eat snack foods in smaller amounts and get healthy, can you? Haub stated that he ate a Twinkie every three hours versus an actual meal. At the time of Haub's experiment, a single 1.5 oz cake had 150 calories, and he would consume around five of these a day, or 750 calories' worth. He would also eat around 1800 calories of other previously mentioned junk food. The average adult male requires 2,000 to 3,000 calories a day, depending on activity levels, to maintain a healthy weight.

Twinkie Guy further claimed that his low-density lipoproteins (LDL), or what we call "bad cholesterol," improved under this rubbish regimen. Even his triglyceride levels, or fatty acids, got better. Therefore, he was consuming less than what he needed so that his body would naturally start burning fat to maintain normal operation and he would lose weight. It's prudent to note he also consumed multivitamins, a daily protein shake, whole milk, and carrots to not starve his system of required micronutrients (which sounds like a little cheating to me since he was claiming to lose weight only on snack foods). This still sounds amazing, doesn't it? Sign me up. Well, not so fast, muchacho. There is a *gotcha* in this story. You see, Mark Haub was being paid by Big Soda itself to make these claims.

In 2017, the Praxis Project, a non-profit focusing on public health, sued Coca-Cola, accusing the company of using deceptive practices, such as promoting biased research, to mislead the general public about the link between sugary drinks and obesity. The Praxis Project vs. Coca-Cola ended in a $2.7 million settlement, with Coca-Cola admitting to no wrongdoing. In the academic realm, misrepresenting the purpose of one's research and using suspicious funding for said research is tantamount to heresy. Shortly after this story broke, a so-called war on obesity was launched by the US government that made sugar and excessive calories an enemy of the state, blaming sugary snacks and drinks for making Americans obese. The war on obesity went about as well as the war on drugs or on crime. It made for great politics but didn't really deliver actual results that positively affect a free society.

> "One small positive thought can change your whole day."
> —Zig Ziglar

Research has found that happier people tend to have healthier lifestyle habits. A study done with over seven thousand adults in Lithuania, ages forty-five to seventy-two, found that those with a more positive mindset were half as likely to eat more fruits and vegetables than the other half who were considered more negative. Let's be honest: a carrot doesn't exactly give you the same dopamine fix as a piece of chocolate cake or a bag of potato chips, but it provides more nutrients.

The reality is food is how we connect with other people (don't jump to section three just yet!). Around the world, food plays a significant role in many different civilizations. It represents their traditions, habits, beliefs, and history. Not only does food provide sustenance, but it also helps to bring people together and provide a sense of unity. Meals associated with major holidays like Thanksgiving, Christmas, Yom Kippur, Rosh Hashana, Cinco de Mayo, and Diwali are just a few examples of occasions all over the world where people come together to celebrate and connect. Food is even viewed in some cultures as a way to communicate with one's ancestors.

Think about your first date. It probably either started or ended with eating food. Wedding receptions normally involve a meal. Americans barbecue on weekends, the Fourth of July, and before football games. Food is a part of human culture. Remember when we time-traveled back to prehistoric times? Your archaic human forebears gathered around the fire in the cave and cooked up some mouthwatering mastodon. It was to survive starvation, yes, but it was to celebrate. To celebrate the hunt, not starving to death, and taking care of each other.

The reality is that people needed to get better educated on nutrition. They still do, but I can help with that.

CHAPTER 3
HAPPINESS REQUIRES LEARNING

> *Happiness is a choice that requires effort at times.*
>
> **—Aeschylus**

Being content with your health depends on having a solid understanding of nutrition since it gives you the knowledge you need to make wise food choices. You can modify your diet to suit your demands by learning about the various nutrients and how they work in the body. You can use this information to make better assessments and stay away from items that can cause unhealthy weight gain and other problems. Planning meals that give the right nourishment for a healthy lifestyle can also be beneficial. I love fish sticks and tater tots, but eating them every day is probably not a great choice overall.

Education about good nutrition will assist you in lowering your risk of developing a chronic illness. You can change your diet to include more of the foods that are good for your health by studying the health advantages of certain nutrients.

Consuming foods high in vitamins, minerals, and other nutrients is a good way to ward off diseases like diabetes, heart disease, and some types of cancer. To ensure you are getting the most nutrients possible from your diet, you need to learn how to properly prepare and cook your food.

Last but not least, nutritional education can give you a sense of having more control over your regimens. Having the information necessary to make wise decisions might help you feel less stressed about your food selections and more confident in your capacity to make healthy choices. When you are aware of the value of nutrition, you are better able to plan your meals and snacks. Additionally, having this knowledge will result in increased emotional stability and lifestyle satisfaction.

CALORIES

> "Calories: tiny little creatures that live in your closet and sew your clothes a little bit tighter every night."
>
> **—Unknown**

What is a *calorie*? A calorie is a unit of measure. It is not fuel for the body; it is how we measure how the body burns its fuel. Specifically, for those more scientific folks reading this, a calorie is the measurement of energy needed to raise the temperature of one gram of water by one degree Celsius (33.8 degrees Fahrenheit) in the body. This makes sense when we talk about *burning* calories. The body needs to burn fuel constantly regardless of what it's doing. It needs fuel to keep the heart pumping blood, the lungs pushing air, and all the other major organs, like the brain, kidneys, liver, etc., operating. Even when we sleep, we are burning calories, just at a minimal rate. Depending upon age, biological sex, and activity level, the human being needs around 2,000 calories a day for normal operation.

American multi-Olympic gold medalist Michael Phelps used to

consume between ten thousand and twelve thousand calories a day when training. That is because his body needed to burn more fuel to maintain the metabolic requirement for Olympic-level swimming and at the speed and intensity at which he was training. Going back to Professor Twinkie's theory that less calorie intake leads to weight loss isn't entirely incorrect, however. What he failed to say is that not all calories are created equal. Again, a calorie is a unit of measure. The *type* of fuel the body burns is what we need to pay more attention to. In the twenty-first century, we have become way more health-conscious than ever before. And with the internet, we can conjure up the information we seek to understand how to live healthier and happier lives. For us to find happiness and longevity through healthy living, we need to dig into the basic science of nutrition.

> "Happiness is nothing more than good health and a bad memory."
> —Albert Schweitzer

Kevin Hall, PhD, a senior investigator from the National Institute of Diabetes and Digestive and Kidney Diseases, took up the mantle of studying *Biggest Loser* contestants' postcompetition after Danny Cahill's victory at the end of the show's eighth season. He led a team of nutritionists, mathematicians, and neuroscientists to better understand the correlation between weight gain and weight loss regarding how we eat and exercise. Dr. Hall argues that calories have increased in our food since the 1980s, stating, "The rise in calories per person is much more than enough to explain the increase in body weight." Calories in food increased up to 800 calories per person, and although we waste two-thirds of our food, that extra one-third was enough to spark an obesity epidemic. This results from more processed foods put on grocery store shelves when food costs increased in the 1970s. Plus, companies have been dueling to have the tastiest food on those shelves, which has also added an increase in preservatives and sweeteners to satiate consumer palates.

What you may not know is that as you lose weight, your body burns fewer calories. Despite this metabolite alteration, you can continue to lose or maintain weight by further altering caloric intake and energy expenditures. If you move less, you may have to eat fewer calories than if you are more active in that same timeframe. However, eating fewer calories can drive up an appetite, and a loss of control could force you to binge eat to meet the needs your body says you have.

NUTRIENTS

> "Our food should be our medicine and our medicine should be our food."
>
> **—Hippocrates**

Nutrients are the substances that we must consume to live, grow, reproduce, and everything in between. Further, we typically break nutrients into two major categories: macronutrients and micronutrients. Macronutrients are classed into three categories: carbohydrates, fats, and proteins.

Okay, let's nutritionally nerd out for a nanosecond. A basic carbohydrate, or carb, is a biomolecule containing carbon, hydrogen, and oxygen atoms. Notice I said *basic* carbohydrate. There are a lot more complexities to carbs that I won't get into only because it would not serve the purpose here of how nutrition leads to happiness. Just know that there is way more science to it than what I'm offering.

Carbs provide multiple functions for the human body, but more importantly, they are central to human nutrition and are found in nearly everything we consume. Specifically, all good things that we eat, like bread and starches—why many diets call for reducing or eliminating bread and pasta from their diets. Carbs provide the primary fuel source for the human brain, heart, and central nervous systems and sustain the digestive system, cholesterol levels, and help control insulin levels.

Carbs are broken down into three main groups: sugars, starches, and dietary fiber. Sugar, also known as a simple carb, gets a bad reputation due to junk food, but sugars are also found in fruits like apples, bananas, and berries and are the easiest to digest. Overindulging in sugar does lead to weight gain and obesity because it is easily converted to fat in the human body. However, there are some health benefits to sugar. The body needs to burn calories to function, and sugar is an easy and quick source of calories to burn for an almost immediate source of energy. It also helps the pancreas modulate insulin, which helps break sugars down in the bloodstream. More easily understood by everyone is that sugar is also a mood enhancer. Let's face it: desserts like ice cream, cake, and cookies all make us a little bit happier. Take heed, however, because sugar is addictive due to the dopamine released after eating it. Remember—everything in moderation.

Starches and fiber are complex carbs and contain many more nutrients than sugars. Starches come from certain foods like potatoes, bread, and pasta, while fiber comes from fruits, vegetables, and legumes. The only purpose for starches is to latterly be converted for energy purposes, while fiber is used to assist the human digestive system. In other words, it's good for your bowels. Never hurts to have a good poop . . . unless you have too much fiber, and then it very well could hurt to poop, and no one enjoys that.

"This is all fine and dandy, but how do carbs work?" you might be saying. Well, I'm glad you asked!

Once eaten, carbs, except for fiber, are broken down into sugars. Carbs are then utilized within the first thirty minutes, which is why it is good to consume some form of healthy carbs thirty to forty-five minutes before exercise. Carbs will only be stored for two to four hours before being converted to fat. This is a holdover from our caveman ancestors that we visited earlier who did not have food readily available and needed fat stores to sustain them over long periods between hunts and during the often-cruel winter months. So, when our rather hairy ancestors lacked food and carbs for near-instant energy, they tapped into their fat stores. Fat is used to insulate the body, specifically vital organs and nerves, as well as help generate internal heat, as each gram of fat supplies nine calories to be burned. Also, fat helps aid in the absorption of certain vitamins like A, D, E, and K.

A quick war story for you. When I deployed to Afghanistan, I worked primarily nights. I flew C-130 transport planes and AC-130 gunships, and the aircraft cannot be seen well at night without the aid of low-light devices like night vision goggles and is therefore afforded a level of protection from enemy threats. I tell you all of this because working nights means seeing the sun a lot less, and the sun provides our most prominent source of natural vitamin D. In the short term, like the three months I would be deployed, vitamin D deficiency caused added fatigue and weakened my immune system. We would all get some form of the "crud" while deployed due to breathing in the dirt, sand, smoke from burn pits, and jet exhaust. Working in close proximity to others and weird work schedules didn't help either. I quickly found that taking a vitamin D supplement every day helped fight fatigue. I still got the crud, but I bounced back faster taking vitamin D supplements versus not.

Vitamins, like those previously mentioned, but also B vitamins, such as B-12 and B-6, help the body to metabolize fat, breaking it down to be used for energy. Now, keep in mind there is a difference between healthy and unhealthy fats. Healthy fats, also known as dietary fats, are a nutrient, just like carbs and protein. They help absorb vital nutrients and minerals for normal bodily functions. We get these from things like nuts, avocados, and peanut butter. Unhealthy fats, called trans fats, raise bad cholesterol and lower good cholesterol. Trans fats come from junk foods and otherwise processed artificial foods. Over time trans fats will cause clogged arteries, which leads to heart disease, heart attacks, and strokes.

I mentioned cholesterol twice already. Once with Professor Twinkie and then just now while discussing fats. It's important to dig just a little deeper into that because it is essential for all animal life, but no one knows what it is until they are told their bad cholesterol is . . . well . . . bad.

Cholesterol is produced in the human liver, and if you were paying attention in high school anatomy class, you remember that the liver helps detoxify the body. Lipoproteins—molecules made up of fat and protein—help carry cholesterol out of the body. Low-density lipoproteins (LDLs) carry cholesterol into the bloodstream, while high-density lipoproteins (HDLs) carry cholesterol out. As I mentioned before, we typically consider LDLs to be bad, though LDLs aren't cholesterol at all, just the vessel in which cholesterol moves. LDLs carry most of the fat molecules through the bloodstream. If the fat manages to be thinned out, then mostly protein molecules remain to make it HDL, or what we call "good cholesterol." Bad cholesterol, or too much fat going into the bloodstream, can create clogged arteries and other heart-related problems. If your bad cholesterol is too high, you need to consult with your physician to get on a proper diet to get those levels down. And exercise! Don't worry; we'll cover that topic in a minute, too.

The last macronutrient, protein, is a vital part of the human diet. We require seven grams of protein for every twenty pounds of body weight daily. It is worthwhile to mention that millions of people across the planet, mainly children, do not get enough daily protein due to food insecurities. The National Academy of Medicine suggests that we make 10 percent to 35 percent of our daily diet protein-based. We get our proteins mainly from meat sources like beef, pork, chicken, and eggs, but there are plant-based proteins for vegetarians and vegans, such as tofu, chickpeas, and lentils.

DIETING: WE ARE WHAT WE EAT

> "It took more than a day to put it on. It will take more than a day to take it off."
>
> **—Unknown**

If you didn't read the disclaimer at the front of the book, I'll reiterate that I am by no means a doctor, nutritionist, or any other type of medical professional. I didn't even stay at a Holiday Inn last night. I'm just an ordinary human being like you, trying to figure out life and be happy. (That is the theme of the book, after all.) We're going to discuss dieting, but please make sure to talk to a *real* medical professional before doing so. Don't be Professor Twinkie.

There are a lot of dieting plans out there. You can download an app on your smartphone that will help you count your carbs, help you meal plan, and figure out what to eat during different times of day. It is remarkable how modern technology can aid your ability to live a healthier lifestyle. A lot of people lean on the popular fad diets, however, like keto and Atkins.

The keto diet is a low-carb, high-fat diet and has become very popular with those wanting to drop weight and body fat quickly. The idea is to keep carbs to only 20 percent or less of your daily caloric intake with the premise that carbs are the source of weight gain and unwanted body fat. While this is technically true, it's more a misconception because only *unused* carbs are converted to fat. The trade-off to low-carb eating is a higher healthy fat intake. Those on keto are allowed to eat larger amounts of fatty foods and proteins like meat and cheese. So, hamburgers with no bun or just a platter of crispy bacon.

You're drooling already, aren't you?

However, because of the low-carb rule, as well as zero sugar intake, certain healthy foods, like most fruits, are off-limits due to their carb contents. And followers aren't allowed to ingest any alcohol either, by the way.

The Atkins diet is very similar to keto, with the exception that those participating are allowed 30 percent consumption of carbs versus 20 percent, which is more conducive to a healthy diet for someone slightly active, though not sedentary. While these diets do have proven effects, there is concern that low-carb diets deny the body much-needed nutrients, although a simple solution to that would be to take a daily multivitamin. How many carbs should you eat? The 2020–2025 Dietary Guidelines for Americans (DGA) suggests carbohydrates should comprise between 45 percent and 65 percent of our total daily calories consumed, based on a targeted intake of 2,000 calories a day. That means, per the DGA's suggestion, 900–1300 calories should be in the form of carbs or 225 to 325 grams.

Another popular weight-loss program, the Beachbody diet, allows up to 40 percent carb intake and balances out the rest with equal parts protein and fat. Unlike keto and Atkins, the Beachbody diet is a fixed-schedule diet over twenty-one days that promises up to fifteen pounds of weight loss. It focuses more on more organic, less processed foods, supplemented with core workouts, rather than focusing on macronutrients.

I feel obligated to tell you that before starting any diet, please consult a physician and go over the pros and cons of these weight-loss plans. While they can show some powerful weight-loss results, there can be some harmful side effects. All three mentioned diets can lead to some severe nutrient deficiencies. A physician may recommend dietary supplements to ensure you're getting all of your required nutrients. Also, keto has been known to put undue stress on the kidneys—even leading to kidney stones—due to higher amounts of uric acid and calcium taken in by high fat and high protein consumption. Another negative of these diets, specifically with the Beachbody diet, is the short-term focus. The dieter wants the fast results of losing up to fifteen pounds or more in less than thirty days, but the Centers for Disease Control and Prevention recommends no more than four to eight pounds of weight loss a month or one to two pounds a week. As we discussed with the Biggest Loser competition, massive weight loss above what is recommended can have negative effects on the human mind and body.

Is dieting bad? Not at all; however, when we often talk about dieting, we refer to fad diets like the keto, Atkins, or Beach Body diets. Dieting is very healthy when done correctly, and there is enough evidence to prove that losing weight does increase a person's happiness by increasing their self-confidence and self-image. But the biggest problem is that we often look at dieting as not eating, starving ourselves to lose weight and excess fat. I'm sure you're familiar with the term *hangry*—the state of being angry or otherwise disagreeable when hunger is setting in. Dieting isn't about *not* eating but eating correctly because it doesn't take a genius to know that food makes us happy.

YOU NEED TO SWEAT TO BE HAPPY

> "No one has ever drowned in sweat."
> —Lou Holtz

If losing weight is part of your happiness journey, then you need to understand something very simple yet so very important. You need to *sweat*.

Ruben Meerman, affectionately known as the Surfer Scientist, is an Australian scientist, educator, author, and speaker who still maintains a glorious head of hair in his fifties. He spent a lot of his work in education, teaching science to children to make it fun and encouraging the next generations of scientists, but as of 2013, he has been working in the realm of weight loss, specifically answering the question of where fat goes when we lose it.

Meerman explains the science of weight loss. Human fat is comprised of water (H_2O) and carbon dioxide (CO_2), creating an actual chemical formula for human fat ($C_{55}H_{104}O_6$). This is a basic construct, as some fat cells may have more or less carbon and hydrogen but, regardless, will always have six parts oxygen. So, Meerman further details that the difference between washboard abs and a muffin top is a bunch of $C_{55}H_{104}O_6$. Okay, I'm not a physicist, a biochemist, or a mathematician, so I won't complicate this more than it needs to be. The bottom line upfront for all of this is that fat leaves the body via carbon dioxide or water. We either sweat it out, pee it out, or breathe it out. This is basic metabolism. However, it's not just an automatic function because, as we talked about in nutrition, your body is always converting nutrients into fuel, either by actively burning it or sending it to storage for later use in the form of fat.

This is important because there are tons of gimmicks out there to convince you of how to lose weight. Just go into your friendly neighborhood health and wellness store that sells overpriced protein powders and shaker cups with your favorite comic book superhero on them, and you can find a variety of pills, potions, and snake oils to convince you that they will help you burn fat. I'm not a scientist, and I won't try to play that there are substances out there that will help you burn that bellicose belly fat because you could smoke meth for a month and probably lose a hundred pounds, but I wouldn't recommend that because, well, meth will kill you. So, don't do that. You can save hundreds of dollars by bypassing a lot of these concoctions and burning fat the natural, healthy, happier way by eating differently and working out.

Since we've been scientific with this happiness thing, let's keep going with that. What happens when you exercise? Well, when you work out, a series of chemicals are released into the brain: endorphins, dopamine, and adrenaline. Endorphins interact with your nervous system and release in response to pain and discomfort by creating a sense of euphoria, like that of opioids, by the way. If you have ever had a runner's high, it's a real thing. As you run and your body is being stretched physically due to strain, endorphins kick in to tell your brain that it's not really in pain, so that it can keep going. This is a naturally occurring phenomenon that our cavemen ancestors we visited a while ago needed to keep fighting threats such as that vicious saber-tooth cat or to keep running after the wounded deer they need to eat. Endorphins also kick in during other strenuous activities or can interact with your nervous system in less stressful activities as well. The same euphoria can normally be achieved when eating decadent foods like chocolate, listening to music, or having an orgasm. All three are a wicked good time.

Another chemical collaborator during exercise is myokine, which is released when your muscles contract during exercise and not only helps you reduce stress but helps to make you more resilient to future stresses.

Find a routine that works for you. You don't have to run ten miles if you don't want to, and don't be afraid to run ten miles if that is your thing. Go for a light jog or even a walk. I have found I can burn just as many calories with a brisk walk as with a run; I just have to walk a longer distance. By the way, this is a great time to listen to some relaxing music or even an audiobook. Maybe even this book? Picking up and putting down heavy things is also great. Weightlifting increases muscle, helps to burn fat, strengthens bones and joints, and improves heart health. You don't have to squat four hundred pounds either unless you absolutely hate your lower back. Start light and work your way up. You can use bodyweight exercises like push-ups, squats, sit-ups, etc. to have similar results. Another important factoid to mention is to shift up your workouts periodically. Your body will become used to the same exercises over and over, and they will be less effective. In other words, your body will get bored.

EAT LESS, MOVE MORE . . .
AND WHY IT DOESN'T WORK

You have probably heard the mantra "Eat less; move more" a lot from a variety of dietary professionals. Even Ruben Meerman makes this comment in a TED Talk about weight loss, discussing the biochemistry of the process previously mentioned. But it's wrong.

This paradigm is based on the theory that body fat is a result of excess energy, i.e., if we take in less energy, we will lose weight. But as mentioned previously, energy, or calories burned, is an output. The theory makes sense at the surface level: if you eat less, then you won't be creating fat, but if you were paying attention earlier, carbs, fats, and proteins are all absorbed differently in the body for different reasons. In the short term, it does work. Caloric deficiencies will have short-term weight loss results; however, the human body has some defense mechanisms that will kick in. Appetite will increase because the body will start craving nutrients it's not getting during fasting periods. And being hungry all the time doesn't make you happy, by the way. When you cave into the cravings and binge-eat a pint of ice cream for the subsequent dopamine fix, the shame of eating so much sugar will take over. Now not only will you not feel happy, but you'll probably have a stomach ache from so much ice cream. Hope you're not lactose intolerant.

If you watched *Sesame Street* or any number of preschool learning shows growing up, you probably heard that breakfast is the most important meal of the day. I can't say if it's the most important, but it does have health benefits. You need to understand that when you sleep, you are in a fasting period because your body is going hours without any sustenance, yet it is still burning calories to maintain bodily functions. This is important to know if you choose to fast because you already have a fasting cycle built into your normal routine. Breakfast, even something small like a piece of fruit or toast, breaks up that fasting cycle, replenishes your glucose levels to give you energy, and kicks in your metabolism. Having told you that, I will admit I am not a breakfast eater. I do like a good brunch on the weekends, though. On average days, instead of a heavy breakfast, I like to snack on almonds or have a protein shake in the morning before having a light lunch. Do what works best for your healthy habits and what makes you happy. I mean, that's the whole premise of this book!

Another quip you have probably heard is that if you don't eat, your body will go into *starvation mode*. The idea is that your body will hold onto fat to make up for the lack of calories being consumed and consequently burned. This is typically considered to be a false narrative. Jennifer Low, a registered dietitian, owner of JL Nutrition Clinic, and a spokesperson for the British Dietetic Association, admits that when your caloric intake is way too low, your metabolism slows down in response. Your body is trying to maintain weight. This will only lead you to be lethargic and frustrated with a lack of weight loss. Rhiannon Lambert, the United Kingdom's leading nutritionist, adds that starvation mode, as we know it, only occurs in extreme nutritionally neglected occurrences and is often associated with eating disorders. The bottom line here is that England's smartest dietitians are saying that starvation mode isn't a thing, but the results are the same. Your body will protect itself because that's what it is designed to do.

Here are some simple things you can do that will help. Eat slower. Hormones control your appetite, the amount you eat, and when you feel full. There is often a twenty-minute gap between when your body is satiated and when your brain is told your belly is full. Eating slower can close that hormonal disparity and help signal faster that you are full and should stop eating. Of course, eating should be an experience anyway. Enjoy your food! Increasing your protein intake will also help by aiding in that hormonal timer and filling you up faster when you eat. Oh, and drink plenty of water.

This sounds like a great transition.

HYDRATE OR DIE

> "Sometimes I drink water just to surprise my liver."
>
> —Unknown

The prehistoric ancestors we visited in our time machine would migrate with the animal herds to stay close to their food source. Another benefit to this was that the animals they hunted would migrate toward water sources for their survival. Searching for water was as easy as tracking the herds. As humans evolved, they established their settlements near major sources of water like rivers, lakes, and oceans. Babylon was built on the Euphrates, all of Egypt around the Nile, and even the state lines of the United States were established around major water sources like the Mississippi, Ohio, and Missouri rivers. Water is imperative to our survival.

The human body consists of up to 60 percent water as a whole. Our brains are 73 percent water, our lungs are nearly 83 percent water, and even our bones are 31 percent water. Needless to say, hydration is an extremely important part of being healthy and something that is often neglected. A 2013 survey conducted by CBS found that 75 percent of Americans are normally dehydrated daily. This is because we consume more soda, coffee, sugary energy drinks, and a myriad of other diuretic beverages throughout the day.

Good old H_2O does everything for our bodies, from helping digestion, maintaining proper brain function, and detoxifying our liver and kidneys. Water increases our energy levels, fights fatigue, and can significantly improve our mood. Ever had a headache that started small, you ignored it, and it kept getting worse? More than likely, it's due to dehydration. In a study done on 102 men, 25 percent to 40 percent showed fewer headaches just by consuming 1.5 liters of water a day.

In the military, recruits are taught to manage hydration based on the color of urine. There are visual charts on the bathroom walls of every US military installation showing the varied colors of your pee so you know if you should be drinking more water. Clear is good, yellow needs more water, super dark—like the color of tea— and you're in trouble! In Air Force Basic Military Training, often called Boot Camp, every recruit carries a one-quart canteen on a belt every day, and training instructors check that those canteens always have water and that their trainees are hydrating. Nothing sucks more than passing out due to dehydration on a drill pad in San Antonio, Texas, in the middle of a sweltering summer. You will not get any sympathy. You will awake to yelling, screaming, and gnashing of teeth. It's best just to keep drinking water regularly.

How much happier will you be if you are in a better mood, less tired, and not suffering from those pesky headaches? Especially if we're talking about improving your nutritional and workout habits, proper hydration is another important aspect of all of that. Also, without water, we would literally die. Most people can go a week or more without food but will die of thirst after three days. So, *not* dying of dehydration will make anyone that much happier.

SLUMBER AND SATISFACTION

> "Let her sleep, for when she wakes she will shake the world."
>
> **—Napoleon Bonaparte**

I have suffered from sleep issues for years. Some of it stems from working weird hours, like showing up to work at one or two o'clock and working until midnight or later, just to get four or five hours of sleep and go back to work at eight or ten o'clock the next morning. Did

I mention I was in the military? That alone should explain it. You suffer through and get by on other facets to get you through the day, like caffeine, nicotine, and sometimes just pure adrenaline. Do this for over a decade and see how devastating it is to the human body and psyche.

The Center for Disease Control found in 2016 that one in three Americans are considered sleep-deprived and typically get less than seven hours of sleep a night, the amount recommended for adults ages eighteen to sixty. Sleep is critical for good health and happiness. Lack of sleep deprives you of alertness and mental concentration and impairs memory, which can be dangerous when driving, operating machinery, and diminishing balance. Falling off a ladder while putting up holiday decorations will not help in your search for happiness. Sleep deprivation leads to poor moods, which affect your relationships with others and diminish your overall quality of life.

I confess this chapter has been much like an eighth-grade health science class. There is a reason for that. Happiness doesn't come from some magical potion, though many of my friends at the local bar might disagree. Happiness—true, unadulterated happiness—comes from taking *action*. You must do the work. I'm giving you the tools in the form of knowledge to do that work, to make that change, to find a happier you. If you made it this far, maybe you can go a little farther with me. Let me continue to take you down the journey because there is so much more to learn.

CHAPTER 4
HAPPINESS REQUIRES TEMPERANCE

> *Everything in moderation, including moderation.*
>
> —Oscar Wilde

EVERYTHING IN MODERATION

Once upon a time, there was a little child who only ate sweets. One day, the little glutton went into an antique store. I'm not sure why, but for some reason, the small scoffer thought he might find something tasty in there. Bear with me.

On his sojourn, the chubby child found a magic magnifying glass that he liked so much that his parents bought it for him. I'm going to go out on a limb and say this young fellow was wildly spoiled, as it seems that all his parents did was feed him candy and give him what he wanted.

This sweet-toothed foodie took his newfound magnifying glass and started looking for things to see. He found an ant that, when viewed through the magnifying glass, appeared much larger, and when he took the glass away, the ant mysteriously stayed as large as it had appeared in the magnifying glass! This little activity thrilled him, and he started experimenting by looking at other objects that would also remain bigger after viewing them through the magnifying glass.

Then, he got an idea! The little glutton ran back home and started viewing his candies through the magnifying glass and then started eating them; now that they were much larger, he had more to eat. He ate until he was so full he could eat no more.

The next day, he awoke swollen with a horrible stomachache and even a tinge of purple, which is concerning since that probably means he had an oxygen circulation issue unrelated to his overeating habits. The doctor was summoned because this was a time when doctors made house calls without the interference of insurance companies, and the doctor said it was the worst tummy ache he'd ever seen in his professional career as a traveling physician. For some reason, the doctor ignored the obvious cyanosis, but again, I'm paraphrasing the story, so don't shoot the messenger.

The bulging boy's suffering was so bad that he didn't want anything to do with sweets or candies or even food in general. His parents were elated because now they could keep the pantry stocked with desserts that wouldn't be immediately consumed by their spoiled little child. The little glutton hid his magnifying glass in a box until he was ready to see things that were worth making bigger. The moral of this bedtime story is that even with the best things in life, too much can hurt you. It's better to experience them moderately.

This is an actual bedtime story told to children, by the way, so please don't get angry at me for calling an affluent child with an apparent eating disorder a "little glutton." It's literally the name of the story; however, it makes a great point. More isn't always better. Too much food will make you ill. Too much house will rack up high utility bills because you must heat it and cool it. Too big a car, and maybe you don't quite fit in those closer parking spaces anymore. Too much sex can make you dehydrated, sore, and . . . we'll stop there and move on.

> "A man must know how to choose the mean and avoid the extremes on either side, as far as possible."
>
> **—Socrates**

Irish author and playwright Oscar Wilde (1854–1900 CE) wrote, "Everything in moderation, including moderation." I'm pretty sure he was just requoting Socrates, who spoke vivaciously on the virtue of temperance. Regardless, this is a bit ironic since Wilde allegedly had a taste for luxury and debauchery.

Temperance has often been discussed regarding an abstention from alcohol, and more than likely, Wilde was being tongue-in-cheek about not drinking as much. The reality, however, is that temperance is not about *not* consuming alcohol. Instead, it is a virtue of not overindulging or going to the extreme with anything, including our actions. But what about underindulging? Is that even a thing, and if so, why would that be bad?

Outside of the Western idea of temperance, meaning abstinence from alcohol, temperance can refer to the self-control of anything: eating, vulgarity, partying, television watching, even sitting in the sun too long. A more scientific view of moderation is eliminating or reducing extremes in either direction of the proverbial plumb line of life. In layman's terms, temperance is self-control, but we'll talk about that in a minute. Sticking with the alcohol-related theme, if you drink a fifth of Fireball a day, you will probably destroy your liver, but if you never partake of the sweet cinnamon nectar, then what kind of fun are you really having? Okay, okay. That one isn't necessarily the best example, I admit.

I fully acknowledge that if my only retort to underindulgence, or not indulging at all, is merely a lack of prodigious joviality, then I fail to make a great case for not partaking in Satan's syrup. But holy hell, if you died living a boring life, did you even really live?

> "And then she went to the porridge of the Little, Small, Wee Bear, and tasted that; and that was neither too hot nor too cold, but just right."
>
> —Robert Southy, *Goldilocks, and the Three Bears* (1837).

The story of *Goldilocks and the Three Bears*, to keep with the children's story theme, is often used as an analogy for that middle ground or "just right" option in life. The porridge she found was neither too hot nor too cold; the bed she laid on was neither too hard nor too soft; and so on. Of course, we omit the fact this girl broke into someone else's domicile, ate their food, damaged private property in the form of sitting on the littlest bear's chair and breaking it, and was caught sleeping in the Three Bears's home and managed to escape with her life. Maybe not being a criminal should be the moral we teach our children with this fairy tale? Nevertheless, this story is meant to illustrate that middle ground we are looking for with temperance.

TEMPERANCE IS A VIRTUE

> "Temperance is moderation in the things that are good and total abstinence from the things that are foul."
>
> —Frances E. C. Willard

The very definition of temperance has evolved over thousands of years, but it maintains a common theme of being a form of self-discipline. One of the earliest versions was control over oneself, focusing on emotions and personal judgments.

The ancient Greeks saw temperance as one of the four cardinal virtues by which everyone should live, the others being courage, justice, and wisdom. Even the Temple to Apollo at Delphi bore the inscription *Medan Agan* or "nothing in excess," showing how elevated the concept was to their society's faith. From pre-Socratic times until the Roman Stoics of Epictetus and Seneca, moderation was part of virtuous living, from a person's diet to exercise, even in how they studied. Aristotle saw temperance as self-control from physical pleasures.

The Latin definition of temperance is like the Greek translation. However, the Latin focuses more on self-restraint in what the Romans called "passions." I am referring to what we typically consider negative emotions like anger, hate, fear, and envy. Marcus Aurelius, one of Rome's most benevolent emperors and a Stoic philosopher, leaned more toward temperance as complete opposition to physical pleasures. Thomas Aquinas, a thirteenth-century Italian Catholic priest, would take that opposition to physical pleasures to a new height by using the virtue as a guard against fornication, alcohol use, gluttony, and anything the Church considered a cardinal sin or a threat to European theocracy.

St. Thomas Aquinas wrote that temperance is "the disposition of the mind which binds passions." His philosophy on temperance was more in the aversion to pleasure more so than pain. Early Christians had some gratification with accepting negative things such as poverty, hunger, and sometimes even physical pain as a sign of spiritual strength and humbleness before God. I would argue that if you are going to practice temperance that it be in all regards, both pleasure and pain. God never commanded anyone to go hungry or whip themselves with a cat-o'-nine-tails while chanting Latin mantras to prove their love to Him.

The virtue of temperance, according to Saint Thomas Aquinas, is responsible for "withholding the appetite from those things which are most alluring to man" or for "withdrawing man from things which entice the appetite from following reason." Aquinas's rationale is that mercy, meekness, humility, and studiousness are connected ingredients that rely on moderation. While temperance is the moderation of physical things, I'm going to argue that moderation in life is more than just regulating corporeal things, particularly as it relates to the pursuit of happiness. While that is important, you must moderate much more to find your eudaemonia.

> "Thoughts Become Words, Words Become Actions, Actions Become Habits, Habits Become Character, Character Becomes Your Destiny."
>
> —Tom Rowland

You need to moderate your thoughts more than anything. As Tom Rowland stated in a December 2021 podcast, "Thoughts become words, words become actions, actions become habits, habits become character, character becomes your destiny." Having complete control of your thoughts is a difficult task—they are your thoughts, after all, and you have every right to them, whatever they may be. The challenge is ensuring those thoughts don't drive you to the point that you feel you must act irrationally on them to alleviate any emotional strain. The reality is that your thoughts are all correct in their own way, but in terms of finding, keeping, and maintaining happiness, we need to focus on the definition a little bit. In my opinion, that definition is *balance*.

WORK-LIFE BALANCE

> "Work, he reckoned, was the best medicine of all. Work is what horses die of. Everybody should know that."
>
> —Aleksandr Solzhenitsyn

Hi, my name is Adam, and I am a recovering workaholic. I used to be that guy who worked an inordinate number of hours, always volunteering, despite my recruiter telling me to never volunteer for anything and was always on the road for my job. Keep in mind my *job* was in the US Air Force, and I flew C-130s for twelve years of my time in the military. Despite the amazing adventures I had, it was not easy on my young family. It took most of my military career to finally start realizing that my proverbial plate just wasn't big enough to take on every task, and when I finally got the nerve to say, "No, I can't handle that task. I already have too much," they just said, "Okay." That was the moment I had an epiphany. Let me walk you through that.

One, never assume your leadership, supervision, management, insert hierarchical system here, knows how much bandwidth you're working with. They are only human, too. Don't be afraid to say, "No. I can't take that on." I would suggest trying to recommend someone who might be able to do it instead to help in their decision-making process; it's a team sport, after all. And if they come down and say, "Nope, this has to get done, and it has to get done by you," then remind them of what tasks, functions, and objectives will have to go on a back burner until that task is done.

Remember this: success is not measured in how many things we get done in a day, week, month, or year. Those can make a good portfolio to showcase your work and highlight a career, but that does not necessarily mean you were successful.

New York Times best-selling author Shawn Anchor, in his book *The Happiness Advantage,* makes an excellent case for why success alone isn't enough to achieve eudaemonia. He writes, "If success causes happiness, then every employee who gets a promotion, every student who receives an acceptance letter, everyone who has ever accomplished a goal of any kind should be happy. But with each victory, our goalposts of success keep getting pushed further and further out so that happiness gets pushed over the horizon."

Have you ever worked an extremely long day? Put in hours of work on a project, task, or objective? Then, after all that time and the effort that you put in, you finally go home feeling like you didn't accomplish a frigging thing. As I approached the sunset of my military career, I started to feel that way more and more. When I was a flight engineer flying the venerable C-130, no matter how bad a sortie got, at the end of the mission when I walked off the airplane, I felt a sense of accomplishment if nothing more than that I had contributed my part in getting everyone back home safely.

Some of my best days were after the most harrowing of missions, with things going wrong left and right, exhausting me both physically and mentally, yet I would watch the sunrise over the mountains near Kabul, Afghanistan, as the dawning of a new day signaled the end of my duty period, and I would feel proud.

PRIORITIZE YOUR HEALTH

> "If you don't take time for your wellness, you will be forced to make time for your illness."
>
> —Unknown

A close colleague of mine was going through some cruel health issues. We'll call her Tiffany. She had gone to the hospital for one matter, which was horrible enough, only to be told she was going to lose her kidney. She spent weeks in the hospital and required numerous procedures. I visited her as much as I could, sometimes twice a day, and was I worrying myself sick over here . . . literally. I wasn't sleeping, wasn't eating, and was surviving on caffeine to get me through the days. It was taking a toll on my own health.

I mentioned something to my wife about not feeling well, and she said, "It's because you're so worried about Tiffany, and you're not focusing on yourself." She didn't mean I shouldn't be worried about Tiffany—worrying is what friends do. But what my wife was expertly pointing out, as she usually does, was that I was of no use to Tiffany, or anyone, if I ended up in a hospital bed next to her because my own health deteriorated from the anxiety I was experiencing. It's the same thing as "Put your oxygen mask on first before you help others." If you pass out before you get the mask on your fellow airline passenger, then you're both screwed.

In the world of military aviation, we have an acronym called DNIF for *duties not including flying*. It denotes a medical status that meant you were either sick or injured and couldn't fly. No one wanted to be DNIF, and a lot of times, we would let ailments go untreated for years to not lose our flying status, even temporarily. A lot of the issue was that we just wanted to fly. It was what the Air Force paid us to do, to go fly multimillion-dollar airplanes, and we loved it. There were other administrative issues too, like flight currencies, proficiency in the plane, and flight pay, that were always at stake when you didn't fly for long periods. For the love of the game, many of us went untreated for different issues for years, only to have it bite us in the ass ten to fifteen years down the road. If we were lucky, we were behind a desk at that point in our careers and could finally take the time to go get seen by flight doctors and properly treated.

At some point, we all realized that as much as we loved flying, at some point, it was going to end. We were going to stop flying or leave the military, and that chapter would be over, and another one would begin. What were we going to look like in that new chapter? Bad backs, bad knees, bad shoulders, hearing loss, impaired vision, cranky, sleep-deprived, and dependent on caffeine and nicotine. A military career is hard on the human body.

> "Sustained exhaustion is not a badge of honor; it's a mark of stupidity."
> —Jason Fried

The sad reality is, at the time of this writing, American culture sees working oneself to utter exhaustion as a measurement of success. I pray that someday the person reading this says, "That hasn't been the case in twenty years or more." In the meantime, society perpetuates this living myth that you must constantly grind away to be successful, happy, and on top of the world. Celebrities get on stage and tell people that you can't sleep eight hours a day if you want to be rich. Rich people don't sleep eight hours a day. You must get up and *grind* and *hustle* until you make it! Make it where? Where is the finish line where you can finally sleep eight hours or more?

This mentality is especially prevalent in the modern workplace. A team can spend days, even weeks, on a project, and in the meeting to announce to the boss that the project is closed out, the words "Okay, here's what we do next" come out. What do we do next? Seriously. Can't I just have a day to appreciate what I've already done? There is this fallacy here that being busy is the same as production. I used to joke when I was in the Air Force that all you had to do to keep from getting tasked with something was walk around the squadron with a paper or a folder in your hand, and the rest of your teammates would assume you already had a task and leave you alone. Even if all you were doing was bullshitting most of the day. For the most part, it worked because there was, and probably still is, a culture in the military that being busy is a positive sign of production, and you're getting stuff done. That's why, after many years, I stopped telling people I was busy and either said I was being productive or nonproductive because that was a more accurate statement. Everyone can be busy, but not everyone can be productive at all times.

Brené Brown, in her book *Daring Greatly,* discusses how she observed technology and the realities of the twenty-first-century economy, creating a paradigm where everyone has more than one job, and there is an unscrupulous adage that everyone must "do more with less." I saw this much of my military career. In fact, *do more with less* became a mantra for nearly a decade as the US military dealt with budget cuts and force reductions while still maintaining a combat presence all over the globe, specifically in Iraq, Afghanistan, and then Syria by 2014. It is not a sustainable model. Eventually, we would hear senior leaders retort with, "We have to do less with less," but in my twenty-plus years, I never once saw that happen. It was the same old "do more" maxim with a feel-good motto. Nothing actually changed.

Even the use of automation and artificial intelligence hasn't relieved you of the burden of overwork and underproduction. While those facets have made life easier in some regards, it didn't levy the workload; it merely shifted your responsibilities to other tasks, often for less pay, as manual labor could be done by software.

Stop glamorizing overworking!

The lack of sleep, bad diet, no exercise, the inability to relax, and zero time with family and friends is not something that needs to be applauded. Don't wear your burnout like a red badge of courage because exhaustion is not a status symbol; it's the body telling your brain to rest. Eliminate from your conscious thought the idea that you must be constantly grinding, hustling, and slaving away to be successful, even if it's your own business. You are bombarded on social media with images of the thirty-somethings who retired at twenty-something because they invested every penny and lived on ramen noodles so they could stop living in a cubicle farm. While I'm sure those people exist, most of the time, it's pure bullshit. You need to embrace the idea that rest, recovery, reflection, and resiliency are important facets of being a successful person and living a happy and healthy life. If you kill yourself to pay your house off early but literally die of a heart attack the day you make the last payment, you didn't do yourself, or anyone else, any good. Take a day and just relax. Read a book, go for a walk, or run. Watch old movies and eat popcorn. Avoid the news for a day or two.

I'm not saying you shouldn't work. I'm not a fan of generational welfare or those who suckle on the teat of the truly successful to avoid getting their hands dirty. We must work to survive, to be comfortable, to find our eudaemonia, but living just to work is just a form of modern slavery. Therefore, balance is the key here.

ALCOHOL

> "Drink because you are happy, but never because you are miserable."
> —G. K. Chesterton

You're probably wondering why alcohol isn't in Chapter One. It affects our health, after all. And you're right; it does. Full confession: Chapter One was getting long-winded, and most of this chapter was birthed from its editing phase. However, alcohol fits perfectly here in the discussion of temperance because alcohol is one of those subjects that broaches many planes of discussion. There is a health piece to alcohol, but there is also a spiritual, political, and even legal aspect to the topic of booze. And it can influence our happiness—on either side of the scale.

A temperance movement started in Saratoga, New York, in 1808 and spread throughout the northeastern United States. Temperance, in this case, was considered abstinence from alcohol. It became a topic of education as well as state and federal legislation for decades, and of course, led to the complete prohibition of alcohol in the US following the First World War. Just for the record, Prohibition in the United States only banned the manufacture, sale, and transportation of alcohol, not consumption. This is often misconstrued when teaching American history. Of course, this ban only led to black-market booze, back-alley bars, and a vibrant moonshining industry in the Carolinas that eventually led to what is now NASCAR. A hundred years after Prohibition, we can see that the United States went through a stark identity crisis. Legislators thought Prohibition would solve social issues, reduce the burden of taxes on American citizens, and keep poor drunks out of jail. It did not do any of those things.

I know what you're thinking: *Great history lesson, Adam, but what does this have to do with alcohol and happiness?* Academic research has shown that responsible, social drinking has short-term positive effects on a person's happiness, while irresponsible drinking has long-term negative effects. Yeah, no shit. Anyone can see that. So, what? Although it is true that alcohol has a depressant impact, it is not as simple as that due to the vast range of effects it has on the human brain. Alcohol may inhibit brain activity in one region, but that area may connect to another area to prevent it from activating; thus, alcohol indirectly raises activity by inhibiting something.

This depressant effect appears to be the foundation for some of the more classic effects, such as reducing activity in the temporal lobes and prefrontal cortex. The prefrontal brain oversees rational cognition, planning, appraisal, and the control of anger—all complicated processes that vanish after a few drinks. You are aware of how alcohol affects memory because memory processing areas are in the temporal lobes, and therefore when you drink, you lose your ability to control yourself and can become more confused and forgetful. But this doesn't explain why you like drinking or why drinking can make you happy—in the short term. Alcohol enhances activity in opioid cells that produce endorphins as well as dopamine neurons in the mesolimbic reward circuit, which may explain this characteristic.

So, drinking alcohol can make you feel happy because of its chemical effects, and not drinking alcohol could make you happy because of the lack of aftereffects of drinking, like hangovers or holes in your walls. Moderate drinking can make you feel happy because you feel like you're in control, and if you're in control, you feel content when you can just shut it off and say no more, or you know you're okay, so you can have another in an hour. Drinking moderately has a positive impact on your mood, so while those pleasure endorphins are kicking in from the consumption itself, knowing you can turn it off and back on again without risking the negative consequences that come with drinking to excess lets you enjoy yourself that much more.

THE POWER OF NO

> "It's only by saying no that you can concentrate on the things that are really important."
>
> —Steve Jobs

Katy was a go-getter, never afraid to tackle a new task or welcome a new challenge. She got straight A's all through high school, graduated Summa Cum Laude from a top ten regional college and earned an amazing opportunity to intern with a major magazine in the United States. Katy was an independent, confident, and extremely intelligent young woman. She was the epitome of what a millennial feminist should be as a role model for young women in modern America. But Katy could not say no to anything. She said yes to every new opportunity to put a larger workload on her plate; every extra task sucked more personal time away from her as she worked sixty to eighty hours a week to meet the demands of her editors. Her life became nothing but work.

Now, before you label her supervisors as some modern-day robber barons burying a young, somewhat naive woman under the weight of the labor force, I want to tell you from my own experiences, that we all have so much going on in our lives, especially at work, that a lot of times our bosses don't know how buried we are. I ran programmed flying training (PFT) for AC-130U gunships in a formal training unit (FTU) from 2016 to 2018. An FTU is a demanding place to work because you are flying training lines, ensuring that training folders get updated and are accurate, and there are normally at least two to three other additional duties associated with each member of the cadre.

On top of that, new tasks pop up within short timeframes all the time, which sucks time and energy away from the primary objectives. In the military, especially in the special operations community, if you are a go-getter like Katy was, and leadership knows you are dependable, they will continue to throw work at you because they know you will get it done. The machine must keep moving. The downside to that level of trust is that if you don't manage time effectively, if you can't delegate appropriately, and you don't have the balls to say, "I don't have the bandwidth to get after this task," it will just keep coming. The point, though, is to not immediately turn your ire to your bosses. They may not actually know how much weight you're carrying because they are busy balancing their own plates on sticks. I will tell you that the first time I had to say, "I can't take on that task. You'll have to talk to someone else," it was liberating and a massive relief when my bosses just said, "Okay. Thanks."

By the time Katy was twenty-four, she had her own office and her own team and was taking on the big stories. She was on her way! Saying yes was paying dividends in her career early on. She'd probably be an editor before she was thirty, a senior editor before forty, and she was becoming a well-known name in American journalism. But she had few friends, no personal life, and the expensive apartment she was renting was barely lived in. She was saying yes to the wrong things, and to too many things, and the weight of her success was starting to bear down.

> "When you say yes to something you don't want to do, here is the result: you hate what you are doing, you resent the person who asked you, and you hurt yourself."
>
> —James Altucher, *The Power of No: Because One Little Word Can Bring Health, Abundance, and Happiness*

There is a movement in corporate America of saying yes to everything for a year, and it is supposed to bring empowerment. Let's assume you are a boss for a moment. When an employee gives you an idea, you are supposed to say yes to it. If the idea fails, oh well, but at least you showed your employee you were willing to hear their idea out and let them take action on it. Saying yes to opportunities is supposed to be empowering because you never know which opportunity is going to be the next big thing or the next million-dollar idea. In the military world, they *say yes to everything* is a squishy idea, meaning it doesn't quite feel right. Now, trying out new ideas, empowering your people, and taking advantage of opportunities are all great things . . . until they're not.

I acknowledge there is more to this concept than just saying yes and rolling out. Risks, time, and resources all still must be managed within a project scope, but I don't want to get into the weeds here on how to run a project. It's to make a point that while not everyone likes hearing *no*, much like our children who may throw a tantrum, *no* can be a healthy thing for everyone. Another mantra in the special operations community is "Find a way to yes." I hate this phrase because it is used carte blanche on what leadership cares about in that five-minute time span. Find a way to *yes* to get the mission done? Absolutely! No questions asked. Kill bad guys and save good guys? Let's roll! Find a way to *yes* to determine how to circumvent regulations to get something done to help a three-star general become a four-star general? No thanks.

It happened all the time, however, and I have no doubt it is still happening in the Air Force. I found that Air Force chief master sergeants (the Air Force's highest enlisted rank) hated it when I used the mantra to ask why they weren't finding a way to stop an airman from moving his family for the fourth time in six years or putting an airman in an assignment where they could flourish as opposed to just making their records look good for a promotion board that they may never see for ten years, if at all.

Just remember, there is power in saying "No, thank you," or "I can't get involved at this time," or "I can't make time for that." It's polite, it's tactful, and it doesn't chain you to something you didn't want to do or can't do at that time.

CHAPTER 5
HAPPINESS REQUIRES STRUGGLE

> *I'm grateful for my struggle because without it,
> I wouldn't have stumbled across my strength.*
>
> —**Alex Elle**

THE STRUGGLE IS REAL

As we discussed in an earlier chapter, when a caterpillar is going through metamorphosis in its cocoon, every step of that process, from beginning to end, must be uninterrupted because every second of the transformation is critical for the butterfly to form. The butterfly must struggle for it to survive. Struggle is essential to your transformation, as well. If whatever process you are going through is interrupted, you may not transform into what you need to be, especially regarding your happiness.

Struggle is inherent in almost anything. For example, a good novel requires a struggle for it to be interesting. The protagonist needs a challenge like solving the mystery, stopping the villain, or saving the world. Maybe all three. The challenge must escalate to some insurmountable difficulty that will quickly turn into an impossible problem to solve. Then, in the end, and against all odds, the hero wins the day via luck, skill, or both. Regardless, without the struggle and the chance for the hero to live or die throughout that struggle, the story will just be plain boring. Even better, if the author can show a level of personal growth and change in the hero as they fight on, then the author can create different hooks to keep the reader attached to the story—maybe even create a connection between the reader and the protagonist as well. It's something we can all relate to because to be happy is something we all need, and to achieve that, we need to face adversity, challenge, and difficulty; we have to struggle. I will show you some things we struggle with in our pursuit of our eudaemonia.

LIFE ISN'T FAIR

> "Life isn't fair. It never was and never will be."
> —John F. Kennedy

A problem we all have is that we expect life to play by some archaic playground rules and be fair to you because you have been fair to others. You're fooling yourself, just like you were fooled into believing you wouldn't be clotheslined playing Red Rover in the first grade during recess. Maybe that was just me? Asking the world to play with such rubrics is like asking a lion to not eat you just because you did not eat it.

Even some of history's most iconic celebrities dealt with life's inequitableness. Bill Gates, cofounder of Microsoft and tech mogul, watched his first business crumble around him; the same happened to Walt Disney, who was told he lacked creativity. The New York Yankees, one of the most successful baseball teams in the world, went bankrupt in 1962; Steve Jobs, the cofounder of Apple, was tossed out of his own company! Milton Hershey had three previous candy companies folded on him before he got it right. Even Michael Jordan, one of the greatest basketball players of all time, was cut from his high school basketball team during his sophomore year. Okay, this isn't entirely accurate. This one is a myth perpetuated to illustrate how life can be unfair, even to the best of us. In reality, Jordan didn't make the varsity squad and was placed on the junior varsity team to get more experience and playing time, but you could see this as being a type of cut. And there are plenty more vignettes like this all over the world of people who struggled to find their success, but more importantly, to find happiness in their success.

That life isn't always fair is one of the first lessons we learn as kids. But most of us still hold fast to the notion that everyone gets what they deserve. The good guy always wins, the hero wins the girl, and the princess lives happily ever after. How about one more example of a myth? Marriage is fifty-fifty. I will cover this more in Section Three, but know that marriage or intimate relationships, in general, are never fifty-fifty.

We may interpret the world as a sequence of transactions because of this worldview, which has enormous effects on our expectations. You should receive a beverage if you put the money in the machine. Work hard, and you will move up the corporate ladder. If you are kind to others, then they will be kind to you. These expectations are not always unreasonable, but they are frequently not satisfied. When you insert your money into the soda machine, it will occasionally jam. Even when you work hard, someone else may get the promotion. Even though you're a good person, there's always some asshole down the street you have to deal with.

Our faith in justice in the world can err toward charmed thinking. For instance, people who frequently use a business think they have a higher chance of being treated better than other customers—a finding known as the *lucky loyalty* effect. Similar reasoning encourages some to believe in karma. Karma, in Hindu and Buddhist faiths, is a principle of causality that basically reasons that if you treat others well, you, in turn, will be treated well, but if you treat others ill, then you will, in turn, be treated ill. Again, while it sounds nice and is a good principle to bind positive values to, it's still bullshit only because we know good things happen to bad people, and bad people still marry hot celebrities and drive Ferraris. There is a downside, however, to believing in universal fairness. Some women who have a strong sense of justice in the world are more likely than other women to place the guilt for a fictitious stranger's rape on the victim. Additionally, those who believe in a just society are less likely to hire a job applicant who has just been previously fired or has had previous criminal offenses.

> "The ego is not master in its own house."
> —Sigmund Freud

In his best-selling book, *Ego is the Enemy*, author and modern Stoic philosopher Ryan Holiday argues that throughout history, ego has gotten in the way of success because ego often leads to putting self-importance on a pedestal, and that ego leads to personal failure. Ego has unquestionably steered some major downfalls in human history. It has cost brilliant leaders their very lives, begotten the downfall of great civilizations, and generally caused a lot of unhappiness and suffering. To understand how struggling in life will make you happier, you need to understand ego a little better, though.

All of us have an ego. It is how you identify with your sense of self and who you believe yourself to be. It exists in your mind as your thoughts, your beliefs, and even how you perceive your values. This is all based on several factors, like where you grew up, for instance. This state is called *ego-consciousness* and is a defensive state of your existence where those thoughts, beliefs, values, opinions, and judgments all become a threat to how you see yourself. This is where your ego finds its importance. However, it is a reactive state where you tend to take the behavior of others personally, and this causes you to suffer. In this state, you create different story arcs about how others acted toward you and how you acted toward them. You inadvertently become the hero or the victim in your story, while others become villains. It is all based on what we consider to be rational perceptions and assigns meaning, even purpose, to the events that surround us. We all do it, and we do it all the time.

The ego-centered portion of the mind is where the need for *more* lies. This is where your need for more money, more success, more love, more free time, more sex, and more happiness lives. The ego is often associated with the behavior of self-importance, sometimes inflated but not always so, or excessive confidence—what we may call cockiness. To some extent, this is all true, but the ego is far more complex than that. No matter what you give your ego, in our psychological maquillage, it will never be content. You can feed it with everything imaginable within your power, but you will never quench its thirst. Imagine the ego as a child who has an abundance of toys to play with and treats to eat but still acts out and demands more. When you give the ego what it desires, it is only content for a brief period before it begins to crave more.

On the road to happiness, getting rid of the ego in your daily relationships is crucial. We've all made choices based on our egos and seen others in our lives do the same. These interactions frequently have harmful and completely unintended results. So why do we, as rational beings, act and speak in ways that we do not intend to? Is it something we're born with or learned growing up? It's the whole nature versus nurture conundrum.

> "You're not as good as you think. You don't have it all figured out. Stay focused. Do better."
>
> —Ryan Holiday, *Ego Is the Enemy*

Think about times when someone doesn't call, text, message, or email you back. You get anxious because you want to hear back from them. It could be a day, it could be an hour, it could be a few minutes, but regardless, you start creating stories in your mind as to why this individual hasn't gotten back to you.

Your brain goes to the worst places: they don't like you; they're hanging out with someone else; you're going to get fired. Maybe it's your significant other, and they're cheating on you with someone more attractive than you. Maybe it's that new job offer that you accepted, and you imagine them retracting that amazing deal they just handed you in writing. It's all irrational because, while those things could very well be the truth, the reality is that you don't know why they haven't responded to you. Then you are relieved when you find out they were napping, in a meeting, their phone battery died, or some other more rational, less threatening explanation comes about. Regardless, for a moment—or longer—you considered the worst-case scenario.

This can cause jealous reactions, as well. Perhaps you see someone doing something you want to do. Or someone else got a promotion or a better job. Maybe someone you know got that new car you've been wishing for. So, your ego goes into a different mode, and you start to get down on yourself, thinking, *I suck! They are so much better than me. I could never accomplish those things; I could never be that good!* If you think that way long enough, you truly start to believe it.

One of my favorite scenarios is what is called the *principal's office scenario*. Remember when you were in school, and you would get that godawful summons over the loudspeaker to go to the principal's office? You didn't know why you were called, and you would start formulating those irrational scenarios in your head about what you might have done wrong. Let's be honest: if you did something wrong, you probably would know why you were called down the hall. Nevertheless, it became the longest walk of your life, only for you to find out your mom had called and you needed to go to someone else's house after school, or you had forgotten your soccer cleats at home.

The ego also creates alternate endings to life events. You get bullied on the playground, and it ends with you on your butt with a bloody nose. You start playing different scenarios in your head where the fight goes in your favor, and you are victorious over your adolescent abuser. Or, my favorite, you argue with someone, and three hours later, you come up with a good comeback that you'll probably never have the opportunity to use. These familiar patterns of behavior start to feel predictable and, therefore, form a safe space for our egos. The ego now doesn't have to grow or evolve because it is within its boundary of what it sees as its identity and will preserve that identity at all costs.

This is where ego becomes a problem. But if we become more aware of how our egos work and more educated on how our subconscious minds work, then we can make the ego a tool for increasing our happiness. It can prevent us from making irrational decisions, knee-jerk reactions, and illogical judgments about ourselves and others. You see, it is never about *us*, and it never was, but our egos will tell us otherwise. The ego will convince us that we are victims, heroes, or villains instead of telling us that we are none of the above. We just . . . are.

Our ego isn't really the enemy. We are not our ego. Instead, the ego is a complicated part of our psyche that helps us make sense of the events that happen around us and to us. It can be our enemy if it is not directed maturely and reasonably. We have a choice in the stories our egos create. This is powerful because if we can steer those perceptions in the right direction, then we will suffer less and find more contentment. For example, we are always concerned that someone will dislike us even if we don't know those people. If you understand—more importantly, if you accept—that others disliking you or just not caring about you at all is a good thing, then you will start to find a more real, authentic self. That fear of being disliked creates an irrational fear because you are being controlled by your ego. To be happy, to be content, to mature and grow as a rational human being, you need to let go of needing to be liked. Embracing your ego doesn't make you a raging narcissist. If you can harness it appropriately, your ego can give you a competitive advantage over your competition—or at least make you less stressed out.

YOU HAVE TO HURT TO BE HAPPY

> "I can't stress this enough, but the pain is part of the process."
> —Mark Manson

If we were to take our time machine back once again to our cavemen ancestors, we would get a glimpse as to why humans feel pain. You use pain to defend yourself from dangerous activities. It's the same reason that parents teach their children that fire means hot and hot means physical injury. Should the baby nevertheless put their hand in a fire or on a stove, the excruciating pain will be so vivid in the child's mind that they will never do so again. While the cliché *what doesn't kill you makes you stronger* is greatly overused, there's a reason for it: it's true. Pain teaches you how to cope with life's unavoidable troubles and sadness, as well as how to acquire the tenacity and grit necessary to persevere in the face of adversity.

Emotional and psychological pain can hurt just as much as physical pain and affects everyone differently, whether it's the devastating loss of a loved one or an accident that leaves you traumatically scarred. Take breaking up with a romantic partner, for example; anyone who has been through it understands how painful it can be. It feels like the loss of the only love you'll ever know in your entire life. With each ending relationship, you realize you're more resilient as you grow and learn.

IMPOSTOR SYNDROME

> "Fear is stupid. So are regrets."
> —Marilyn Monroe

One of the biggest issues with writing a book is the feeling of being a fraud. I'm no stranger to these feelings and have struggled with thoughts like, *No one will read this. It's the biggest piece of shit and makes no sense whatsoever*. Well, maybe some of that was probably true of the first draft, at least. But these feelings are typical when we struggle with imposter syndrome, and it can affect any of us.

Impostor syndrome can be a powerful catalyst for constant improvement. It's challenging to feel like you don't have the correct job even when you do, so impostor syndrome can be a potent stimulus for continuous growth. The impostor syndrome sensation frequently acts as a self-perpetuating negative feedback loop. You are tempted to succumb to it, gripped by the fear that the old routines and habits that got you here won't work in a new environment. Impostor syndrome can be simple to ignore and pass by without giving it a second thought. However, it can also hinder your ability to advance. It may make you worry about what other people will think.

Impostor syndrome also has an impact on how you interact with other individuals. Even though our thoughts are genuine and from the heart, you might have trouble believing they are true. You may become fearful of failure or afraid to venture beyond your comfort zone if you feel unworthy of the prize. How can impostor syndrome be avoided from making you doubt your ability to succeed in both your job and personal life?

How we feel and think about ourselves is a measure of our self-esteem. It influences our decision-making, interpersonal interactions, and self-perception. The ability to act with confidence and drive to accomplish our goals and needs depends on having a strong sense of self. It also encourages us to take on challenges and have confidence in our abilities. Sadly, sometimes the things we do to improve our health and happiness might make us miserable. This frequently occurs because of our unrealistic expectations or our excessive emphasis on reaching a certain objective.

For instance, if we set an impossible goal like losing ten pounds in a week, we could give up if we don't succeed. In this situation, it's crucial to stand back and put our attention on the benefits of our health and happiness. We may change the way we think about our objectives so that they are more attainable, and we can concentrate less on the objective itself and more on the progress we have achieved. It's crucial to keep in mind that self-esteem is a combination of how we feel about ourselves and what we do. Self-care techniques, such as getting adequate sleep, eating well, and making time for yourself, can help boost our self-esteem.

GRIEF

> "Sometimes closure arrives two years later, on an ordinary Friday afternoon, in a way you never expected or could have predicted. And you cry a little, and you laugh a little, and for the first time in a long time... you exhale. Because you are free."
>
> —Mandy Hale

Grief never ends; it evolves. It's a thoroughfare and a passage but never a place to hang your hat. Grief is also not a sign of weakness or frailty. It is not a lack of faith in a higher power or love; however, grief is the price we pay for that love. For you to genuinely understand that you may be joyful again, the grieving process must be worked through and given time to take its course. It can take some people a long time to progress through the stages of grief, which includes hope and a desire to experience enjoyment again. A grieving individual needs to deeply comprehend that it is possible to feel joy once more without demeaning the deceased. It can be quite challenging to even have the desire and motivation to explore ways to find happiness after you have experienced a significant loss.

You may, at times, feel like you may never experience happiness again. A traumatic occurrence can include losing a loved one, a career, or a relationship. Those who are going through a life-altering event frequently feel like life cannot continue. But it's possible to regain your sense of joy. Even if it's likely that nothing will ever be the same, it is still possible to recover and rediscover life. There is a process people go through and a means to go back on the road to happiness again, according to several experts.

Take it from me and understand that it is true when I say that you must allow the grief process to complete itself. Do not rush it. You can't expect to be completely happy again until the depth of your sadness lessens. Work through your arcane shame, severe suffering, deep sorrow, ferocious rage, and all the other feelings that come along. A grief counselor can often provide you with a structure for carrying out this work. When a loved one passes away, for instance, some individuals concentrate on themselves, what they can do to find happiness once more, and even devote their time and energy to loving and living for their children or the rest of the family.

Sometimes, it takes something fresh to help lessen the ache when you can't fill the vacuum in the same way. Learning to live again could occasionally call for a change in your perspective and way of thinking, whether it's the personal fulfillment of reaching goals, spending more time with family, or taking up a new pastime. Keep in mind that surviving life after loss is rarely an easy journey. Although nothing will ever be the same again, being different can also be a good thing.

GROWING UP ON THE PLAYGROUND OF LIFE

The playground is the ultimate analogy for growing up. The slide, the merry-go-round, monkey bars, sandbox, see-saw, playing tag, red rover, tether ball, and encountering the inevitable playground bully. Life has its ups and downs, just like on the playground. You will meet friends and foes, learn how to share the load and understand the importance of tenacity and perseverance. You will feel happiness and sadness, achievement and failure. It might be enjoyable to collaborate with others to accomplish a shared objective, but there will also be moments when you feel alone and alienated. The secret is to learn how to deal with disappointment and turn it into a force for future success. Life may be an exciting journey filled with adventures, much like on a playground, so it's crucial to remember to enjoy yourself and the voyage.

HAPPINESS REQUIRES SELF-CONTROL

> "Happiness is an inside job."
> —William Arthur Ward

Picture the following scenario: you're driving to work on a beautiful morning; the sun is shining, and birds are chirping, although you can't hear the birds over your radio blasting out your favorite tunes. There is a tumbler filled with the most delicious coffee in the world; it's a bit too hot right now but will be just right when you get to work. Traffic is heavy but still moving, which is always a blessing. You got plenty of sleep, you're wearing your favorite work clothes with your most comfortable shoes, and it is going to be a great day. Then . . . (insert evil laugh here).

Out of nowhere, another motorist appears, speeding up next to you and cutting you off, coming what feels like inches from hitting your front bumper and causing a bad accident. They speed on, in, and out of traffic to the tune of honking horns. You had to jerk your wheel to prevent a collision. The tumbler of hot, delicious coffee is now on the passenger-side floor, and your blood pressure is now through the roof. You didn't even have time to honk your horn or give the bird to the jerk before they sped off, pissing other people off in the process. How rude! What was that guy, girl, unaccompanied minor driving without a license, doing? Are they drunk? Are they late? Why are they driving like that? If nothing else, they are at least inconsiderate and acting unsafe.

Now you're mad. Cursing aloud to no one in particular, further upset that you are unable to retrieve your coffee leaking all over your car's previously clean floor. By the time you get to work and retrieve what's left of your coffee, you're angry at the whole world. That thoughtless individual just ruined your day before it even started! Or did they? I'm going to let you in on a secret. You may already know, especially if you didn't skip a previous section. Either way, I'll bear all for the sake of all our souls. Ready? Here goes:

Life isn't fair.

That's it! Life isn't fair.

It never was, and it will never be. It's fun to be optimistic and live in the fairy tale land of good things happening to good people and bad things only happening to bad people. Well, folks, it's all bullshit because that's just not how life works. Bad things happen to good people, and good things happen to bad people and every other frigging thing in between. Mostly because *good* and *bad* are values that either we as individuals or we as a society label things or people based on behaviors.

The Stoic philosophers I mentioned before had a very realistic outlook on life. They saw nature as something we have no control over. Not one once of control. Whatsoever. They viewed nature as this cosmic conglomeration of natural sciences and the mystics, seeing both as the same, but that nature, the universe, God, pick one, had its own rules, and we weren't in on them. We just had to play the game. Now, that doesn't seem fair, but remember the little secret I just told you? Life isn't fair? Yeah.

Remind yourself of that constantly when things are going to shit. Remind yourself of that when things are going grand, as well. The best, most educated, most honorable people on the planet have met horrifying demises while the dirty, lowlife cockroaches of humankind are banging someone hot on a bed covered in hundred-dollar bills. That's just the way it is. But that doesn't mean we just stop living or stop being good people. If mankind just gave up trying to find good, be good, and define good then the world would be an even shittier place than it is now without the light at the end of the tunnel or any silver lining whatsoever. Well, then, what the hell do we do? Well, we focus on only that which we can control.

DICHOTOMY OF CONTROL

> "There is only one way to happiness and that is to cease worrying about things which are beyond the power or our will."
>
> **—Epictetus**

If you have the last say, what will you decide? It marks the start of everything. The most crucial question you must ask yourself is, "Who do I want to be?" After answering that, you can decide on the best course of action. Your body, mind, heart, and spirit are the building blocks of who you are and everything you want to achieve; therefore, you must pay attention to the ideas you feed yourself.

The *dichotomy of control* is a Stoic philosophical belief that some things are in our control and others are not. That's it, you say? Yup. It's more like most things are out of control, and only a few things are in. This provides the mental architecture to help in everyday problem-solving. Segmenting problems gives you a foundation for effectively resolving them. Things that you can influence and things that you cannot. So, let's break this down. You oversee keeping the commitments you make to yourself, trusting your instincts, being the best version of yourself, and keeping an eye on yourself. Because the ability to act in accordance with what you desire is at the foundation of self-love and self-worth. To truly achieve what you want, however, it may be necessary to set aside immediate fulfillment in favor of delayed gratification.

If the fact that wealthy people achieve three-fourths of their daily goals isn't a precise indication of what self-control can do for you, then what is? What if, in addition to money, we extend the definition of wealth to include things like improved relationships with others, an enhanced sense of purpose, and wholesome physical and mental health? What if we had the self-awareness to sit down with ourselves, review our performance, pinpoint areas that need development, and then take specific action to improve those areas? All these components need practically daily effort.

First, let's look at the things we have no control over whatsoever, like other people, the asshole driver we talked about before, the traffic jam that he or she caused, the economy, the weather, disease, and conflict. Now, you're thinking, *Well, I can affect those things.* Not really. You can take a different route to and from work to avoid that traffic, but you can't prevent that speeding motorist from slamming into an unsuspecting minivan and causing a massive pile-up that will last for two to three hours. You can save money and pick the right stocks, but you can't influence how the S&P 500 is going to act this week. (If you can, it's probably illegal, and you should keep it to yourself before men in black suits come to visit you.) You can get vaccinated and wear masks, wash your hands, and use enough hand sanitizer to disinfect a battleship, but that won't stop cancer. You can carry an umbrella, but you can't stop it from raining.

Okay, well, what can I control then? Great question. You can control your thoughts, opinions, actions, beliefs, values, perceptions, and interpretations of the actions, beliefs, opinions, and values of others.

DON'T TAKE IT PERSONALLY

> "There is a great amount of freedom when we stop taking things personally."
>
> —Unknown

In *The Last Dance*, a docuseries about NBA superstar Michael Jordan, he frequently admits when he took things personally. From losing MVP to rival Charles Barkley in 1993 to issues with the Chicago Bulls management to the trash talk of other players—his own teammates and his rivals—MJ took a lot personally. However, he took that energy and ran with it. Using his angst and ire to fuel his game on the court was a constructive way of using that energy. I would argue, however, that not everyone is Michael Jordan, on or off the basketball court, and not everyone has the gift to use umbrage so effectively.

There is a myriad of reasons why you might take things personally. You misread what others say or take things literally because you are insecure. It is rather simple to misinterpret what someone else says, particularly when there is a communication breakdown. When you take something personally, you are typically defending yourself. This indicates that you believe that your personality, skills, knowledge, or accomplishments are under attack. Nobody likes to hear unpleasant things spoken about them. It's crucial to keep in mind that everyone has the freedom to express their thoughts, regardless of whether they are accurate or not.

As discussed with the dichotomy of control, you do not influence what other people do or say; all you have control over is how you respond. This is particularly true for the things that you choose to internalize and ignore. You take something personally when you internalize what was said or done, and it fuels false, self-defeating notions. It may also keep you from pursuing objectives for which you have a strong sense of passion. Therefore, you need to learn how to stop taking things personally.

I took a trip to a well-known theme park in central Florida. I think you can guess the area. I should probably preface this paragraph with the fact that I hate crowds, especially when it is shoulder to shoulder. It is bad enough that people in electric scooters and those pushing strollers run over you every twenty seconds, but when you're getting pushed and shoved in a mass gaggle of tourists, the fight-or-flight response comes out. Now, in retrospect, those people were doing what I was trying to do . . . get out of the damn crowd. They were trying to stay with their group and keep their children under their watchful eye just as much as I was. They truly meant no harm. But in one incident, a gentleman pushing a double stroller through a huge crowd and running into people in the process dared to yell at a woman doing the same thing. This pissed me off, and I went off on the guy. Telling him how big a jerk he was, a hypocrite, and fighting the urge to draw off and punch this guy in his smug face.

I didn't, thankfully, but the moral of the story here is that he took what the woman did personally, and I took what he did personally, and the situation escalated faster than a bibbity-bob— oops, I'll stop there so as to avoid a lawsuit.

That example is a bit on the extreme side, but it felt therapeutic to tell it. Let's tone it down a bit. What about if you get a new haircut and no one notices right away? Or you ask a question and don't get a response as fast as you'd like. Or what if someone was just trying to give you a bit of constructive criticism on your work, some solid feedback to help you improve, and you just took it as *you suck*?

OVERTHINKING IT

> "Overthinking: the art of creating problems where none existed in the first place."
> —Unknown

When you repeatedly think about the same thing or scenario until it interferes with your life, that is overthinking, also known as rumination. The two main types of overthinking are dwelling on the past and fretting about the future. Overthinking can make you feel stuck or prevent you from moving forward at all and may create a challenge to focus on anything else. Unable to push the thoughts from your head, your overthinking can worsen certain situations.

Now, overthinking is not the same as being concerned, anxious, or even stressed about a certain circumstance. Short-term focus on a difficult situation may prompt you to act. For example, feeling apprehensive before an important presentation may inspire you to work swiftly. You will put a lot of work into the project and leave a bit early on the day of to make sure you arrive at the meeting on time.

Many people deal with the widespread phenomena of self-rejection. It is the act of depriving oneself of affection and consideration on merits. Low self-esteem, interpersonal issues, and a lack of ambition can all be symptoms of self-rejection. It's crucial to spot the telltale signals of self-rejection and to strive diligently to do so. Recognizing and then actively working against self-rejection is the most crucial step in overcoming it. This might involve engaging in self-care practices and positive affirmations to increase self-confidence. It may also entail resisting self-rejection-related negative thoughts and substituting more uplifting ones.

Self-compassion exercises and an emphasis on one's strengths are also beneficial. Spending time with others who admire and appreciate you is also vital, as is being aware of the language you use when talking to yourself. Self-rejection might hinder us from having a healthy and optimistic attitude toward life.

Recognizing that you are ultimately responsible for the decisions you make is the first step toward taking accountability for your errors. It might be challenging to blame yourself for your errors, especially when things don't go as planned. Although it might be alluring to point the finger at other people or outside forces, accepting responsibility for your errors shows maturity. You may start to move past the error and toward a better result after you acknowledge your responsibility. It's essential to keep in mind that making errors is a normal aspect of being human.

Everyone makes errors. Personal development means we must learn how to forgive ourselves for them. You may take action to make things better and move on without feeling burdened by guilt by adopting a forgiving attitude toward yourself. You may learn from your errors and avoid making the same ones again by owning up to them and accepting responsibility for them.

Finally, it's necessary to keep in mind that while you cannot change the past, you can influence your future. Taking responsibility for your errors is vital, but so is learning from them. For personal development, thinking back on what went wrong, changing your behavior, and aiming to do better moving forward can be helpful.

Overanalyzing the past may be quite damaging. Regret and a sense of powerlessness may result from it. Rumination and negative self-talk are some potential consequences. Concentrating on the now and the future is the greatest strategy for avoiding this kind of thinking. We can begin to see patterns and behaviors that we might wish to modify when we concentrate on the now and the future. We may start preparing to achieve our goals and setting goals.

We may advance favorably by acting and making little improvements. It's vital to keep in mind to concentrate on the variables under our control. Although we cannot go back in time and alter the past, we can learn from it and improve the present. By establishing constructive objectives and making strategies to achieve those intentions, we may take action to change our future. Making little but significant modifications to our routines and way of life can help us move closer to our objectives.

Finally, it's critical to be aware of our thoughts and to know when we are ruminating or overthinking. Stress and anxiety can be lessened by taking some time to unwind and practice self-care. It might be beneficial to change our perspective by taking the time to express appreciation and notice the good things in our lives.

PATIENCE IS A VIRTUE

> "Have patience with all things, but first of all with yourself."
>
> —St. Francis De Sales

On a typical Sunday morning, I'm up early with a cup of coffee and my laptop in my lap, either writing or analyzing my stock portfolio or online shopping. My laptop is my baby. I protect it like it's my third child. I would defend my laptop with my life! Okay, that's a bit dramatic, but you get the point. With all of that said, one Sunday morning, despite being extremely careful, I still managed to spill coffee all over my precious computer.

Let me set the scene. The laptop is on a TV tray near my couch in the living room. I have just sat down on my comfortable reclining couch with ten ounces of Arabica breakfast blend coffee, two teaspoons of sugar-free caramel macchiato creamer, and a well-toasted blueberry-filled breakfast pastry, lightly buttered. The coffee is temporarily on the TV tray, just six inches from the laptop, only long enough for me to adjust a pillow before I move the food and beverage to a safer distance from my electronics and enjoy the sweet early morning snack. The pillow that I am moving strikes the white, porcelain coffee mug perfectly on the handle in such a manner that the mug does a swift 180-degree turn in the air and lands perfectly on my laptop. I'll refrain from the vulgar shrieks that succeeded this occurrence.

I carried that laptop like an infant without a diaper, peeing all over the house. In this case, it was hot coffee dripping off the computer all over the floor into the kitchen in a vain attempt to remove the hot liquid that had already made its way under the keyboard and trackpad. Within minutes, neither of those worked. I could still cry thinking of how expensive that little accident became.

What does any of this have to do with patience, you ask? Well, patience can be considered another underlying theme of this book, but patience is an underlying and important theme for life. I will tell you that I was not blessed with the gift of patience. The good news is that with a little work and a little practice, you can improve your level of patience. Let's get back to my story. Like a wounded vagabond, my wife drove me twenty minutes to the nearest electronics store with a tech help desk. Now, we often torment these individuals in Western society; we call them *geeks* and *nerds*—that is, until our prized electronics no longer work, and then we expect these mild-mannered Clark Kents to turn into Superman and save the day. When this Clark Kent opened the laptop, and coffee seeped out of its artificial pores onto his countertop, he wouldn't even remove his glasses, let alone don the red cape of a superhero to save my day.

Was this a bad day? Not really. It was a bad morning. Maybe. I had a few hours of inconvenience at the store, maybe a few days of inconvenience before my replacement laptop arrived. But my Krypton did not explode, Metropolis didn't fall into evil hands, and I got to spend the rest of the morning having a lovely brunch date with my wife. There are far worse things that could have happened.

Regardless of the result, working hard to attain a goal may make you feel happy and accomplished. It is reassuring to be reminded that we are capable of great things and that, in the end, our efforts will be rewarded. In the end, working hard to accomplish a goal might result in a stronger sense of accomplishment and purpose, which can increase happiness.

Fighting through adversity can teach you priceless lessons about who you are and make you appreciate the good times even more. It can aid in bringing our sense of self-worth and resiliency into sharper focus. This may result in a happier attitude toward life and a more upbeat outlook on the world. We may learn more about ourselves and improve our ability to handle the wins and mistakes that life brings us by struggling to achieve our goals.

This can result in boosted self-esteem and a happier outlook, both of which can contribute to our lives being happier. In addition to motivating us to strive for higher and better goals, going through tough times can help us gain a deeper appreciation for the good times and may enable us to better see our potential.

SECTION II

WEALTH

CHAPTER 6
GROSS DOMESTIC PROSPERITY

> *Any person who contributes to prosperity must prosper in turn.*
>
> **—Earl Nightingale**

Being wealthy can make you happy in many ways. The first way is that it gives you financial security and the ability to live a comfortable life. With financial security, you have the freedom to pursue whatever activities make you content, whether that is traveling, investing in hobbies, or simply having the freedom to enjoy life without worrying about how to pay your bills.

Being able to help those around you is another way that being affluent may make you happy. When you have the resources, you should use them to assist your loved ones, friends, and even complete strangers. This can take the shape of monetary contributions or just being of assistance in any manner you can. Being wealthy can enable you to do things that will make you prosper and be satisfied, including helping others and giving back to those in need.

Finally, having money can make you happy by enabling you to indulge in your interests and aspirations. Having the money to do something can make you feel very accomplished and happy, whether it's starting a business, taking a dream vacation, or following a career you've always wanted to pursue. If you are looking at how wealth, or at least your definition of wealth, can make you happy, please read on.

GROSS DOMESTIC PROSPERITY

> "It is neither wealth nor splendor; but tranquility and occupation which gives you happiness."
> —Thomas Jefferson

Award-winning Jamaican singer, songwriter, and US Army veteran Bob Marley (1945–1981) was worth $11.5 million when he died of cancer in 1981. Yet, his last words to his son, Ziggy, were, "Money can't buy life." One can speculate he was talking about the failure of modern medicine to cure his skin cancer since he could afford the most effective treatments at that time. He could also have been trying to impart to his son that you can't buy your way into happiness with material things. While this is very much surface-level thinking, I would like to think Marley's last words to his son had a much deeper meaning.

But the best things in life are free! This is still true, so I want to be clear here about what I mean when I say *you need wealth to be happy*. I don't mean you need to be rich or otherwise affluent to find your eudaemonia. Affluence is subjective anyway. Materialism doesn't always bring long-term happiness, but living in a van down by the river or a cardboard box under a bridge isn't exactly thriving either. There must be, excuse the pun, a happy balance. Wealth, regardless of size, equals *freedom*. Enough money, which is very subjective, can grant freedom, while not enough can make you less free. At that point, you become trapped in the daily grind of going to work, earning the paycheck, paying the bills, and trying to find ways to catch up on things like home repairs and car repairs.

Just like there are millions of videos of some sculpted twenty-year-old telling you that your diet and workout regimen sucks and you can only succeed in your health goals if you listen to him, there are just as many out there telling you how to get rich. They'll give you the best stock picks; tell you how to buy, flip, and sell houses; and point out what side hustles you can pull off to help pay your rent. (Writing a book is one way, in case you were wondering.) I started trading in the stock market in 2018 and got heavy into investing in 2020 during the pandemic, as everyone else was stuck at home binge-watching ten seasons of some show I didn't care about. My mornings were dedicated to reading, watching videos, and learning the ins and outs of investing.

I have watched many of the videos I have told you about. For the most part, those individuals mean well. Their advice isn't bad so much as it's not an epiphany either. If I buy a house and then either rent it out or just sell it for more than what I paid for it, I can make money. Umm . . . yup. Makes sense to me. If I buy a stock for ten dollars and then sell it for eleven dollars, I make a profit. Umm . . . also, yup.

There are some out there whose advice isn't that great. Those that are pumping up crap stocks are hoping millions of their viewers will buy that stock to push the price up so they can sell it at a grandiose profit with no care of whether you get out of that trade alive or not. Or some otherwise poorly contrived get-rich scheme that will only drive you down to the poorhouse and kick you out of the door without even the courtesy of slowing down.

I'm also not a fan of those multi-millionaires yelling at you, calling you stupid because you got into some debt. You reached out to them to help you get out of debt, not to be berated. They know who they are . . .

If you're still reading, that means you want me to get on with why I think we need wealth to be happy. Thank you for your patience. Let's dive into that.

FINANCIAL HAPPINESS FOR OURSELVES

> "The lack of money is the root of all evil."
> —Mark Twain

Hebrews 13:5 tells us: "Keep your life free from love of money and be content with what you have." Money is the second most mentioned topic in the Christian Bible, with the word *money* specifically stated eight hundred times and discussion of finances, in general, mentioned around two thousand times. Even the various authors of the Bible, and Jesus himself, knew that money is essential to mortal living and that debt is a bad thing. In fact, one of the most famous of Jesus's quotes is, "Render unto Caesar what is Caesar's and render unto God what is God's." This came out of an attempt by the Pharisees, the Jewish religious leaders of the time, to entrap Jesus into bad-mouthing the Romans by saying that people shouldn't pay taxes. On the contrary, Jesus said you should pay your taxes to whom those taxes are deserved.

Financial satisfaction is essentially a psychological condition. It results from knowing you have the resources to buy the items that will improve and simplify your life. Though money might increase your happiness, keep in mind that this effect is limited. It is crucial to have enough money to cover your fundamental necessities, according to research. Beyond that point, however, acquiring more money does not significantly improve your quality of life. Only when it is used properly can money, a resource, make you feel better. On the other hand, not having enough resources will introduce a level of stress that greatly impacts your happiness.

Financial stress is the state of worry or anxiety brought on by money, debt, and other expenses. According to a survey conducted in February 2022 by the American Psychological Association, money is a major source of stress for 65 percent of participants. Younger individuals, as well as adults who identify as Black or Hispanic, have higher percentages. Financial stress is one of the most pervasive and persistent types of stress. Being under constant financial pressure for years can make managing your mental health challenging. Between 2020 and 2023, the United States faced a global pandemic, recession, and the highest inflation rate in the previous forty years.

Although we all know in our hearts that many things in life are more important than money, when you're having financial difficulties, worry, and stress may rule your world. It can undermine your self-confidence, cause you to feel imperfect, and make you despondent. Your mind, body, and social life may suffer greatly if financial stress becomes excruciating.

Financial difficulties may have a significant negative impact on your mental and physical health, your relationships, and your general quality of life, just like any other cause of excessive stress. Your quality of sleep, self-esteem, and energy levels can suffer if you feel defeated by money problems. It can intensify mood fluctuations, leaving you feeling angry, humiliated, or afraid, and lead to tension and disagreements with people closest to you. It can even raise your chance of developing anxiety or depression. Many turn to harmful coping strategies like binge drinking, misusing drugs, or gambling. Financial stress can, in the worst cases, even lead to suicidal ideations. However, no matter how terrible things appear, assistance is accessible.

There is sometimes a tremendous desire to keep things bottled inside and attempt to handle your financial issues alone. You may even view talking about money as taboo and should never do so in public. I was taught to never talk about money outside of the immediate family. You can feel uncomfortable discussing how much money you make or spend, guilty about past financial missteps, or ashamed of not being able to support yourself or your family. However, holding things within can only increase your stress. You'll probably discover that others are far more empathetic to your issues when so many people are hurting financially through no fault of their own.

> "Whoever said money can't buy happiness never paid for a divorce before."
>
> —Anonymous

Contrary to popular belief, money is a much bigger factor in divorce. There are several elements to consider when discussing divorce, including how money impacts divorce rates in the United States. Arguments over money are the second most common reason for divorce, behind adultery. When it comes to conjugal finances, having a lot of debt and having bad communication about that debt causes worry and anxiety. Money is the main source of conflict for close to half of the couples who have debts of fifty thousand or more dollars, and almost two-thirds of marriages begin with debt. It is normally in the form of student loans, car notes, and credit card debt.

The other third of those who dispute with their spouse about money confess to concealing purchases because they are afraid that those things purchased won't be liked and thus cause an argument. If you believed that infidelity was limited to engaging in a sexual or emotional affair with another person, you might want to reconsider because financial unfaithfulness is a real phenomenon. When you don't fully reveal your debt to your spouse or have other signs that you haven't been honest with them about your money, this is referred to as financial adultery. Relationships are created on trust, and conflicts arise when such trust is betrayed. The best course of action is to be upfront and honest about your money

You may think that financially distressed couples are more likely to get divorced. However, being extremely wealthy can have a similar impact. Wealthy couples typically experience financial hardship despite having a bigger family income because of their higher monthly expenses. These expenses may make it more difficult for them to save for their future requirements, including retirement. When this happens, a marriage is put under even more stress. Another way that money affects the divorce rate among rich couples is the fact that one spouse commonly earns more and typically comes into the marriage with a bigger net worth, and as a result, one partner feels inferior.

The best advice is to get premarriage financial counseling, and when you as a couple find yourselves struggling during the marriage, seek a financial adviser and a marriage counselor. A breakdown in communication between a couple has to be addressed before eudaemonia can be achieved.

> "Debt is the slavery of the free."
> —Publius Syrus

I find that many people like statistics and facts, so here are some about the average American credit card debt. In the first quarter of 2022, there were 537 million credit card accounts in the United States, an increase of 6 percent or thirty-one million from the first quarter of 2021. Also, in the first quarter of 2022, credit card debt reached $841 billion, up $71 billion from the first quarter of 2021 but down from the last quarter before the COVID pandemic of 2020, when it reached $893 billion. Further, in the first quarter of 2022, the typical credit card holder owed $5,769, up from $5,611 in quarter one of 2021. The debt burden was highest for individuals seventy-five and older, about $8,100, and lowest for those under thirty-five with $3,700. By the end of 2022, as inflation hit a forty-year high, credit card debt had jumped 15 percent, reaching a twenty-year high in the United States.

Paying down debt is important for several reasons. First, carrying a lot of debt can be a financial burden. If you have high levels of debt, you may find it difficult to make your monthly payments, which can lead to financial stress and difficulty paying for other expenses.

Second, high levels of debt can also impact your credit score. Your credit score is a measure of your creditworthiness and is used by lenders to determine whether to approve you for a loan and at what interest rate. If you have a lot of debt, it can lower your credit score, making it more difficult to get approved for loans or credit cards and leading to higher interest rates when you do borrow. Finally, paying down debt can help to improve your financial security and stability. When you have less debt, you have more disposable income available to save or invest, which can help to build a financial cushion and provide a greater level of security in case of unexpected expenses or financial setbacks.

> "There are two ways to be wealthy—to get everything you want or to want everything you have."
>
> —Ryan Holiday and Stephen Hanselman, *The Daily Stoic*.

What if I told you that the level of happiness in correlation to money starts at seventy-five thousand dollars? Meaning, if you make that a year in income, then your level of emotional and psychological well-being becomes the baseline at that point and starts to increase as that income increases. Dr. Daniel Kahneman, an Israeli psychologist and notable economist, cowrote a study along with professor Sir Angus Deaton, an Anglo-American economist from Princeton University, on how income affects people's emotional well-being.

When discussing subjective well-being, both scholarly and popular conversations commonly raise the question of whether money buys happiness. The subject has been covered in a sizable body of contradictory study material evaluating personal well-being. Kahnerman and Deaton surveyed more than 450,000 US citizens between 2008 and 2009 about various topics regarding their subjective health. They discovered that emotional well-being and life appraisal, two abstract psychological states, are what lead to happiness. Their finding was significant because it gave researchers a fresh and more practical perspective on happiness. The terms *life assessment* and *emotional well-being* refer to various feelings. A broad perspective of a person's entire existence is necessary for life appraisal. The research of Drs. Kahneman and Deaton demonstrates that people estimate their lives based on a retrospective of their accomplishments, even though life evaluation is influenced by the emotions of the day, and that they're more likely to have a positive opinion of their life if they've reached their goals, are financially secure, and are emotionally fulfilled.

The most widely reported conclusion of all the significant and fascinating findings made by Kahneman and Deaton's research is that people with an annual household income of seventy-five thousand dollars are as content as it gets. More precisely, respondents to questions about life appraisal and emotional well-being are less accurate for people with annual household incomes below that. Even though their life evaluation rating keeps rising, those with annual household incomes above seventy-five grand don't necessarily have better levels of emotional well-being. It appears that a seventy-five-thousand-dollar salary is the apex of the happiness bell curve because, according to Drs. Deaton and Kahneman, there is a myriad of reasons why having more money might not make you happier emotionally. One is that people quickly adjust to the things that money can purchase. A fifteen-bedroom mansion with a swimming pool, bowling alley, and ten-car garage is exciting the first month you live there, but after that, it becomes just a house.

FINANCIAL HAPPINESS FOR OTHERS

> "Wealth is only a source of happiness when it is used to good for others."
> —Denis Waitley

If you are an American who has gone through the American public education system in the last thirty years, you were probably required to read F. Scott Fitzgerald's *The Great Gatsby*. It is one of the great American novels, but I fear the lessons being taught in American schools aren't the real lessons we should be taking from the book. For example, Fitzgerald suggests that the American Dream is just that, a dream, and completely unattainable unless you already come from affluence. This brings us to the main moral of the story: money can't buy you friends or love. If you haven't read the novel, I'll give you a synopsis but—warning—there are spoilers ahead. Jay Gatsby, an American World War I veteran, accumulates his millions by bootlegging during prohibition, gaining his wealth in hopes of winning back his former lover, Daisy Buchanan, who is married to an old-money millionaire.

Fitzgerald allegedly told Earnest Hemingway that "The rich are different from you and me," to which Hemingway purportedly retorted, "Yes, they have more money." This is an apocryphal tale reportedly pulled from Fitzgerald's 1926 short story, *The Rich Boy*, in which Fitzgerald gives his interpretation, via literary allegory, about America's affluent caste. This is much in line with *The Great Gatsby* in how he felt about the rich.

> "Money does not buy you happiness, but lack of money certainly buys you misery."
> —Daniel Kahneman

It is certainly true that helping others can bring a sense of fulfillment and happiness. There are many ways that you can use your money to help others, such as donating to charitable organizations, volunteering your time and resources to support causes you care about, or using your financial resources to support friends or family members in need. By finding ways to use your money to make a positive difference in the world, you can not only help others to find happiness, but you can also find happiness and fulfillment in your own life.

There are many ways that wealth can be used to improve society. Some examples include:

- Donating to charitable organizations that work to address social and environmental issues, such as poverty, disease, education, and climate change
- Investing in companies or organizations that are making a positive impact on society, such as those that are environmentally sustainable or that promote social justice
- Using your wealth and influence to advocate for policy changes that will benefit society, such as supporting legislation that promotes equal rights or protections for disadvantaged groups
- Using your wealth to support social entrepreneurs who are working to create innovative solutions to pressing social and environmental challenges.

By using your wealth in these ways, you can help to make a positive difference in the world and contribute to the well-being of others.

Wealth can be understood in terms of the material resources and assets that a person controls, such as their home, car, and other possessions. It can also be understood in terms of financial resources, such as cash, investments, and property. Net worth is often used as a measure of wealth, as it reflects the total value of a person's assets minus their debts and liabilities. In addition to these material and financial forms of wealth, some people also view wealth in terms of intangible resources, such as knowledge, skills, and relationships. These intangible assets can contribute to a person's overall sense of well-being and can provide opportunities for personal and professional growth and success.

In various communities over time, wealth has been defined and measured differently. Money is the most widely used metric for assessing wealth in contemporary culture. However, it offers a simple common denominator for comparison. The amount to which outside factors can affect the value of money can have a major impact on evaluating wealth in this way. Therefore, it's best to look at other things that make people feel wealthy. For some, wealth is measured in time—time spent with family, on a hobby, or just time away from work.

In the United States, financial illiteracy is becoming a much bigger issue, which is particularly true for minority groups in lower socioeconomic sectors. Only 57 percent of American adults are financially knowledgeable, per a 2022 Standard & Poor's survey. Four fundamental financial concepts, risk diversification, numeracy (the ability to understand numbers), inflation, and compound interest, were used to gauge financial competence. The average American's capacity to achieve their financial goals is severely hampered by a lack of financial knowledge. By 2019, only one in four Americans could translate a tax form, and further, one in four Americans would end up defaulting on student loans. Why isn't finance being taught in American schools?

Part of the problem is that the retirement system has changed. In the modern world, there are a variety of retirement options like 401ks and Individual Retirement Accounts (IRA). But from the 1950s until the 1970s, when these types of retirement plans were introduced, workers got a job that they worked at for decades and retired with a pension and other awards. With some exceptions, such as the US military and other government jobs, those days are no longer feasible and are long, long gone. Further, and more depressing, due to the antiquated architecture of the educational system—public and private—there aren't many experts that instruct financial literacy in the US anymore. Unfortunately, a lot of teachers are unprepared to teach financial literacy to the next generation because they lack the necessary understanding themselves. The educational system continues to be heavily weighted toward disciplines like math and science, as those are most desired by post-secondary schools. This has had secondary effects because this has meant that generations of Americans have gone without learning about personal finance or retirement and are therefore unable to teach their children at home. Hell, I could barely help my thirteen-year-old with his math homework!

Some claim that consumerism is the more nefarious cause of the absence of financial literacy instruction. Higher interest payments to banks, corporations, and others result from having more debt. However, I would argue that if the borrower can't pay their loan, then the banks aren't getting their money either, but everyone likes a good conspiracy theory. Nevertheless, the 2008 housing crisis, also known as the Subprime Mortgage Crisis, was caused by financial institutions dropping rates and lending money to everyone, regardless of whether they could pay their loans back or not. When interest rates rose and the value of homes did not, people could neither afford the loans they had due to the 2008 Recession nor could sell their homes for what they owed. The financial institutions that had levied the loans became greedy and took advantage of Americans, and it not only hurt homeowners but did reputable damage to America's financial sector. Ultimately, people on either side of the lending desk didn't know any better.

This has resulted in many Americans becoming intimidated and refraining from raising important inquiries about their financial situations. You are simply taught that to put a roof over your head and survive, you must have money. Despite the numerous arguments for and against teaching financial literacy in schools, there are resources accessible to aid in improving financial literacy and your financial situation. Some benevolent independent financial advisers are committed to promoting financial education and awareness to assist you in developing your abilities and making wise financial decisions.

WHY SHOULD YOU INVEST?

> "The individual investor should act consistently as an investor and not as a speculator."
> —Benjamin Graham, *The Intelligent Investor*

Let's face it: money makes the world go around, and there are two primary ways to make money. The first method is to earn an income, either by working for yourself or someone else. Simple, right? The other way is to invest in assets that increase in value over time, such as real estate, bonds, mutual funds, exchange-traded funds (ETF), and stocks. All of these, or a combination thereof, help generate income. There are others, such as cryptocurrency, art, and certificates of deposit, but what I want to work with you on here is investing in stocks and ETFs. If done correctly, patiently, and meticulously, then you can create a truly passive income stream for the rest of your life. Making money while you sleep is the ultimate flex.

WHAT INVESTING IS AND IS NOT.

> "An investment in knowledge pays the best interest."
> —Benjamin Franklin

What is investing? It is the process of investing money or capital with the specific goal of making a profit or earning more money. Investing simply means putting your money to work for you; it's not very complicated. In essence, it's a different approach to considering how to generate income. Most of us were taught that the only way to make money is to find a job and work. And many of us do just that. There is one significant issue with this: if you want more money, you must put in long hours of work. If you own your own business, you will have to sell more goods or services. Investing, however, is not gambling. Gambling is wagering money on a result that is unclear in the hopes of winning money, like cards or dice. Games of chance. However, the way some people utilize investment instruments can contribute to the confusion between investing and gambling. A stock purchase based on a "hot" tip you heard at the office water cooler, for instance, could be compared to making a wager at a casino. The so-called meme stocks obtain popularity among retail investors via social media. Meme stocks typically gain their popularity from traders sharing them on websites. Young and inexperienced investors frequently purchase these stocks as investments. Unfortunately, some more experienced investors prey on these individuals by hyping up the stock, getting more investors to buy in so that the price of that stock goes up, and then they sell before the "bubble" pops.

One outcome of amassing wealth can be a desire to pass assets down to future generations to keep them in the family. Wealthy people sometimes use life insurance to increase their after-tax inheritance and leave their heirs with more money. A life insurance policy can be utilized as a tool for investing or just to add to your financial security. Even though life insurance isn't just for the wealthy, everyone should consider having some sort of life insurance policy. One is to ensure your family is cared for in case of your demise, untimely or not. Also, if an entrepreneur co-owns a company, life insurance can help pay for a buy-sell agreement in the case of the sudden death of one of the owners. A key person insurance plan might be advantageous for a family business as well. This is insurance for the important individual in a small company, who is typically the owner, the founder, or key personnel.

If an important employee dies before a successor is found, a key person policy prevents the company from failing. The company itself is the beneficiary and can use the money for things like hiring and training new staff, paying off outstanding debts from the business, or covering ongoing operating costs.

Life insurance is more than just a death benefit; it is a way to set up generational wealth, especially for the nonaffluent. There may be a cash value or intrinsic value depending on the type of insurance policyholders. A characteristic of specific permanent life insurance policies that provide lifetime coverage is cash value accumulation. As a result, the insurance can be sold as a life settlement when it is no longer required. Whole life insurance can provide consistent, tax-free income when properly set up. This implies that, if required, an additional income stream could be provided by your policy. Additionally, the insurance policy's cash value accrues over time and can be borrowed against to cover lifetime needs like education bills. Finally, whole life insurance guarantees your death payout regardless of your future health. This is crucial for ensuring the family and successors of the policy owner have long-term security. High net-worth individuals or anyone looking to use life insurance as an investment strategy may find value in each of these advantages.

Wealthier people might be inspired by the associated prospect of tax benefits or the chance to utilize life insurance as an investment, but as mentioned, almost everyone can profit from having it. For instance, regardless of net worth, you might require life insurance if you have a spouse or one or more children; you are your household's main source of income; you have a dependent with special needs; if you cosigned debts, such as mortgages, vehicle loans, or student loans; or want to leave money behind for funeral and burial costs. When assessing your alternatives for life insurance, think about your main justifications, the amount of coverage you anticipate needing, and what policy works best for you and your family. You may choose the finest policy to suit your needs and financial circumstances by researching the top life insurance providers and obtaining quotes online. Overall, taking away the stress of potential financial issues in the future will help add to your eudaemonia.

WHAT ARE STOCKS?

A stock is a piece of a company. When you buy a share of any company, you legally have now become a shareholder of that organization. There are some rights to this, such as voting for board members, etc. So, how does this work? I'm glad you asked.

Let's say you want to open a hotdog stand. You do all the things necessary to start this small business, such as draft a business plan to get a small business loan from your local bank or credit union. You scout out the right spots to sell your hotdogs, such as downtown on Friday and Saturday nights where people are coming and going from the bars or at the local high school for the home football games. You purchase all the licenses, the cart, the umbrella for the cart, the food, condiments, and even a credit card reader because who carries cash anymore? And you're off! Business is booming! You're selling hotdogs like they're going out of style. Chicago chic dogs, BBQ chili dogs, chili dogs with queso, maybe even a faux Fenway Frank. You even upgrade your cart to carry some beverages. And while you're making a profit, you're finding it hard to make the kind of revenue you want to expand and create your own hotdog cart empire.

You decide, after some well-sought-after financial advice from someone with a degree and certifications in giving said advice, that you want to take your little company public, and you go with what is called an Initial Public Offering (IPO). This means you are going from a private company to a public company, so you can sell shares of your company to the public and bring in extra revenue from the sale of those shares of your stock. We can get into the process by which stock prices are determined later, but for the sake of this exercise, let's say that the powers that be determine that each share of your hotdog cart business is worth ten bucks. So, hundreds of people start buying shares.

Now you have thousands of dollars coming in. You use the money to buy two more carts and put them in all the popular parts of town—there is one at every sporting event and even at outdoor concerts. People love your hotdogs. Now the powers that be decide that your stock is worth fifteen dollars a share, then twenty dollars! You're rolling in the dough . . . or dogs . . . now! After a while, people start to get kind of tired of your hotdogs. It could be for any number of reasons: you haven't expanded your variety; sporting events are seasonal, so there are not enough customers; or there is some vegetarian movement taking over your consumer base, and hotdogs are no longer en vogue. The stock price drops to five dollars a share. Now, you're still making money, and you still have thousands of shares being bought and sold in the system. It's just that each share isn't worth as much as before. Well, you'll have to do something about that. Maybe expand into food trucks that sell more than hotdogs, start a hotdog delivery service, or expand your consumer market.

SMALL, MEDIUM, AND LARGE?

The typical investor will have to choose what size companies to invest in if they want to outperform the general market by picking individual stocks or mutual funds. When discussing size, we typically refer to market capitalization. Market capitalization is calculated by multiplying the number of shares a firm has outstanding by its share price. Larger businesses typically carry less risk than smaller ones. Smaller businesses, however, frequently have greater room for expansion. For instance, a corporation with five million outstanding shares and a share price of $20 has a market value of $100 million.

Companies may be referred to as large-cap, mid-cap, small-cap, mega-cap, or even micro-cap. Although the distinctions between each group can vary, you'll see them organized as follows—mega-cap: $200 billion or more; large-cap: $10 billion to $200 billion; mid-cap: $2 billion to $10 billion; small-cap: $250 million to $2 billion; and micro-cap: less than $250 million.

Starting with the market cap, you get a rough notion of where a company is in its business development. Is it, for instance, a recently established public company? If so, there may be room for development. After all, going public is often a decision made by businesses to gain access to investor cash for expansion. A company's market cap can also give a general indication of its stability. Mid-cap corporations are typically more resilient to volatility than small-cap companies, while large-cap companies are typically less subject to market fluctuations than mid-cap companies. These are generalizations and do not ensure that any specific small-cap company will succeed or that any specific large-cap company will weather a downturn successfully. Market capitalization can still be a helpful metric, especially when it comes to diversifying your portfolio. By dividing up your investments, diversification aims to reduce risks such as stocks and bonds, and within asset classes, you can diversify as well.

> "Happiness is not in the mere possession of money; it lies in the joy of achievement, in the thrill of creative effort."
> —Franklin D. Roosevelt

I find the quote by FDR about finding happiness in achievement and creative effort rather ironic, seeing how the majority of his presidency was during the Great Depression and 78 percent of the

American people lived below the poverty line. Regardless of politics, Roosevelt was correct that pleasure isn't just about having money; it's about what you do with it. Do you support charities? Do you leave a large tip at restaurants? Do you assist your surviving mother in paying her taxes? Even while the world isn't depending on you to end world hunger, I think we can all agree that the good deeds you perform for others make any amount of money, no matter how little, worth it. Are you using your money to find methods to live and prosper, which is the very meaning of eudaemonia, or are you just using it to get by?

SECTION III

LOVE

CHAPTER 7
RELATIONSHIPS AND HAPPINESS

> *To touch the soul of another human being is to walk on holy ground.*
>
> —Stephen R. Covey

SOCIAL CREATURES

In 1938, Harvard started what has become the world's longest study on happiness. Some 724 males were studied every two years, with two distinct groups being formed for the study. The first group was made up of Harvard sophomores, not all affluent but well-off enough to get into an Ivory League university. The second were adolescents from Boston's most impoverished neighborhoods. Some from the latter group didn't even have running water.

They were given questionnaires, medical checkups, and interviews to see how they changed physically, mentally, and emotionally over the course of their lifespans. These men went on to various occupations—some served in the military, others became doctors, lawyers, and tradesmen, and one even became president of the United States. (Fine, I'll tell you. It was John F. Kennedy).

By 2016, sixty participants were still alive and actively participating, even well into their nineties. Two thousand children of those original 724 are also now a part of the eight-decade study that will likely see a centennial. What did these researchers find after nearly eighty years of dedicated and deliberate study? What did they find that tells us what makes people happy?

The answer was healthy relationships.

Though it can be argued that since the study is ongoing, there is no "conclusion" per se, it can easily be resolved that close and healthy relationships are key to an individual's sense of contentment. The stalwart researchers found that those participants who were able to maintain lengthy, nourishing relationships with a spouse and other family lived longer and stayed healthier than those who did not. Researchers further found that loneliness depreciated an individual's longevity, and additionally, those who chose to stay in conflicted relationships, such as bad marriages, were also found to have had negative effects on their mental and physical well-being even more so than those who were divorced. For some, that may seem common sense, but for others that comes as one hell of an eye-opener.

Psychologists from Brigham Young University conducted a more modern study on loneliness utilizing studies dating back to 1980 through 2014. Their findings, like those of Harvard, were that loneliness and social isolation increased mortality consistently across genders, geography, demographics, and health-related data.

The research also agreed that as the participants got older, loneliness only enhanced the chance of death. Loneliness can literally kill you. This is proven when looking at cases of American prisoners of war during the Vietnam War, where American service members literally "gave up" psychologically and died in their sleep due to years of isolation. Years of dehydration, malnutrition, and torture only added to their malady, leading to the prisoners passing away.

To further drive the point home, the Centers for Disease Control and Prevention has also declared loneliness a national health hazard. Further, the National Academies of Science, Engineering, and Medicine published a study in 2020 where they announced that more than one-third of adults over the age of forty-five suffer from loneliness, and a quarter of senior citizens over the age of sixty-five are considered socially isolated. Social isolation is being in a deeper state of loneliness associated with a lack, or even complete absence, of social interaction, close relationships, and any context of social support. This leads to a variety of health risks like depression, dementia, and a slew of other physical and psychological maladies that are known to lead to shorter lifespans and a general lack of happiness.

This is further evidence, backed by scientific research, that happiness requires healthy, close social interaction with friends and family. So, to find your eudaemonia, you must seek out and take hold of wholesome relationships. Being a hermit out in the north Maine woods for thirty years away from the stupidity of human civilization may seem placid, but despite mankind's shortcomings, we need each other.

> "Humans are social beings, and we are happier, and better, when connected to others."
> —Paul Bloom

Human beings are social creatures. We have survived for thousands of years by sticking together in groups, tribes, clans, family units, and societies. Psychologists agree that the social nature of humans is an instinct characteristic born within us, and while the Hollywood image of the lone-wolf rambler who needs no one has a dark, romantic feel to it is just a Hollywood fallacy to entertain the masses. I cannot beat the drum enough that there is enough scientific evidence to prove we need healthy social interaction to become and stay stout and happy. Further, these social interactions also require a certain level of affection and intimacy.

In 1944, Dr. Rene Spitz, an Austro-American psychoanalyst, conducted an experiment on forty newborn babies. The research was to determine the effect that affection, and the lack thereof, had on human beings. Half of the infants were given basic physiological needs such as feeding, bathing, and changing their diapers but no other physical attention past that.

The caregivers were instructed to not touch or talk to the children past what was necessary for those basic needs. The other half gave what we would consider normal caregiver attention, such as holding them to comfort them, talking to them, and being overall nurturing. Keep in mind that this was the 1940s, and humans did some dark, jacked-up things in the name of science in those days.

The study ended after just four months, mainly because half of the infants in the first group, the "bare minimum affection" group, had died. The deceased children were healthy, and there was no physiological cause for their untimely demise. It was determined that they had just . . . given up. With no affection and extremely limited social interaction, it could easily be argued that loneliness killed these poor kids.

This was further proven by the hundreds of American prisoners of war during the Vietnam War. Lack of social interaction, lack of affection, and loneliness will not only severely hamper our ability to be happy and reach eudaemonia, but it can literally kill us.

RELATIONSHIP WITH OURSELVES

> "The relationship with yourself sets the tone for every other relationship you have."
> —Jane Travis

The relationships we have with others are proportional to the relationship we have with ourselves. The best way to improve our relationships with others is to improve ourselves. Set standards.

People tend to spend more time alone after the age of thirty, especially if they are not in a long-term relationship or don't have children.

What does your heart have to say to you about love? What about loving oneself? Many of us have pondered this subject at various points in time. Some of us have given up on trying to provide an answer. It's not unexpected that those of us in relationships take time to reflect on our love for ourselves. I'm going to discuss what I consider to be the most crucial relationship fundamental. If you learn to love yourself, it follows that you can love someone else. Even if a relationship doesn't work out, learning to love yourself makes it possible to discover love again.

We must take the time to recognize our fantastic selves when it comes to self-satisfaction. We tend to concentrate on the aspects of ourselves that we dislike, but it's crucial to acknowledge and value the qualities that make each of us special. We might pause and consider the qualities in ourselves that we value. These characteristics might be anything from our behavioral qualities to our physical characteristics. We may also rejoice in our successes. The labor and effort that went into reaching our goals, whether it was something minor, like passing an exam, or something significant, like receiving a promotion, should be acknowledged.

By taking the time to acknowledge and value our accomplishments, we may feel more fulfilled and at peace with ourselves. Additionally, it's critical to allocate time for enjoyable activities. This may be anything from attending a yoga class to reading a book. We may become more present and aware of our best traits and achievements by engaging in activities that make us feel good about ourselves. It is crucial to take care of yourself. We can feel better if we take the time to nurture our bodies, brains, and souls.

Your daily mental conversations with yourself are known as your *inner dialogue*. A constructive or healthy internal conversation promotes self-assurance and aids in overcoming anxiety and despair. Negative thoughts or increased emotions of shame may result from an improper internal conversation. Consider paying attention to how you converse with yourself during the day to foster a positive inner conversation. Do you place more emphasis on events that go well or those that go wrong? Next, try to focus on being grateful. You may start to cultivate a general thankfulness habit by concentrating on your life's positive aspects. It's normal for worrying or pessimistic thoughts to occasionally surface. It could be beneficial to hunt for proof to disprove your pessimistic beliefs.

Putting value on your advantages might boost your self-assurance. Being kind and patient with oneself may be made easier if you acknowledge that you have room for improvement. Consider compiling a list of your advantages. If you find this difficult, think about asking your loving friends and relatives what they think you are capable of. You might also get assistance from a mentor, life coach, or mental health specialist in figuring out your special qualities and how to work on acquiring new talents.

RELATIONSHIPS WITH OTHERS

> "Happily ever after is not a fairy tale. It's a choice."
>
> —Fawn Weaver

While there are a lot of jokes about newfound freedom after a divorce, especially if that marriage was anything but happy, the reality is that divorce is a tumultuous event, extremely emotional, expensive, and anything but happy. The Canterbury Law Group of Scottsdale, Arizona, provided some interesting statistics on divorce rates in the United States. According to their website, up to 45 percent of first marriages averaging eight years will end in divorce, while second marriages are as high as 60 percent! Third marriages are much worse at around 73 percent. It is easy to see that the more times someone is married, the more likely they are to get divorced again. Around 20 percent of both men and women have been divorced at least once, and men and women between the ages of twenty and twenty-four are the most likely demographic to get divorced. Only 6 percent of those who remarry stay married.

According to the National Center for Health, the overall divorce rate in the United States for 2019 was around 37 percent, down from a devastating 50 percent in previous years. A lot of time, marriages, or monogamous relationships in general, don't work because, with the use of the internet and our handy-dandy smartphones, we have the unscrupulous ability to text or otherwise message an ex-boyfriend, girlfriend, or lover in the middle of the night without our current significant other knowing. Facebook is cited as being one reason that 25 percent of couples argue, while social media activity has caused one in seven married people to contemplate divorce. Online affairs, regardless of whether they lead to physical affairs or equally devastating emotional affairs, lead to a third of total divorces in the United States.

Fifty years ago, we weren't sending duck-faced sexy selfies or pictures of our genitalia to others that we were not in a trusted or dedicated relationship. We didn't have another option lined up when things weren't going our way or a "side piece" because we failed to communicate with the person we were already with. Our grandparents and parents generally were married for forty or fifty years or more because they communicated with one another, dedicated themselves to one another, and didn't force their spouse or partner to compete for their love and affection. My parents had been married for over fifty years before my father passed away.

The truth about marriage is that it is the most wonderful thing and the ugliest thing, depending on the moment. When you're dating or just friends with benefits, you don't always see the darkest parts of someone, but when you're married, you do. You see them when they're bitter and angry, stubborn, and even when they're unlovable. You will fight over petty things, like doing the dishes or picking up socks off the floor in the bedroom. But, despite that, you still see parts of the spouse that others will not. You will clean up their vomit and rub their back when they're sick and pick up the slack for their inability to get the kids from soccer practice. And they'll do the same for you because you are partners.

> "By all means, marry; if you get a good wife, you'll be happy; if you get a bad one, you will become a philosopher."
> —Socrates

Marriages aside, how we spend time with other people in general changes as we age. Speaking in averages, in your childhood years, before the age of twenty, you spend more time with those you consider "friends" or at least close associates. However, after you turn thirty, your circle shrinks, and while you may have a lot of people you consider friends, you only hang out or associate with a handful of them.

Also, after the age of twenty, you start to spend less time with your parents but will spend much of your time with coworkers, probably because you will spend much of your adult life employed . . . hopefully. Let's talk about when you become a parent. Before the age of fifty, you will spend most of your time, after coworkers, with your children, and then that time tends to die off. Of course, the time spent with a partner, spouse, or long-term significant other will increase until one of you passes away.

SETTING BOUNDARIES

> "A lack of boundaries invites a lack of respect."
> —Unknown

For successful relationships and self-care, limits are crucial. Limits entail being aware of, respecting, and advocating for your own needs and boundaries, as well as establishing boundaries with other people and educating them on the importance of saying no. You may live a life where you feel secure, respected, and in charge of your own decisions by setting limits. By setting limits, you may guard against being taken advantage of and avoid misunderstandings and damaged feelings. Healthy boundary-setting will enhance your relationships and give you a sense of confidence and control.

We can take care of ourselves and respect the rights of others by setting loving but strong limits. Think of healthy boundaries as a white picket fence adorned with lovely flowers that surround a serene piece of property. A gate and a warm arbor are there to welcome visitors. The gate opens to admit the good and shuts to exclude the dangerous and harmful. When we need to go inside to recharge, the gate closes after we have expressed ourselves and given to others. The gate opens to show gratitude and love, to express acceptable rage or sadness, or to request assistance. Sometimes we simply need to focus on a major endeavor without distractions, so we lock the gate.

Boundaries are frequently viewed as a barrier to keep people out. They do, however, serve as a reminder to respect one another and ourselves. To be at our best, we must express what we need and desire. It is our duty to take care of ourselves and communicate what is best for us. So why don't we create boundaries more readily if doing so is so crucial to our happiness? The simplest response is dread. We frequently worry that we won't be appreciated or that someone may become angry at us. The only person who can truly comprehend what you need and desire is you.

RELATIONSHIP FAILURES

There are three reasons why intimate relationships fail: an irrational need for self-gratification (selfishness), a lack of real intimacy, and failure to communicate, which also leads to the first two instances.

Relationship partners frequently have varying wants and expectations. One may become selfish and disregard their partner's wants if they place too much emphasis on their own needs. Resentment and a breakdown in communication may result from this. You may need to look deep inside yourself to make sure your feelings are genuine. Perhaps your needs are being met, but your thinking is too restrictive. The variety of perspectives your spouse offers to the discourse is one of the lovely benefits of being in an intimate relationship.

One of the symptoms of selfishness is when you regularly find yourself unable to consider someone else's point of view. If you change the way you think, you can stop being selfish in relationships. Do you shut your partner off when they have a differing opinion? Are you so certain that the way you see things is the "correct" way that you refuse to consider alternative viewpoints or even consider them? So, if you become aware that this is what you have been doing, all you need to do is engage in active listening and resist making a snap judgment about your partner's point of view.

Do you assume responsibility when you are wrong or not? This is an annoying trait of a selfish personality. A simple "I'm sorry; I was wrong" can help you move past a miscommunication. If you are in a relationship and are unable to express that, you are being selfish. Do you accept your partner as an individual and the uniqueness that individuality brings? Selfishness in the relationship is evident if you find yourself striving to mold your partner into someone different from the person you fell in love with. If you catch yourself doing this, you need to consider whether you would welcome an effort on your partner's behalf to alter you as well.

Do your needs come before your partner's needs? Making sure you have what you need to thrive and feel authentically you is one thing, but disregarding your partner's wants and needs is quite another. When you continuously put yourself first in a relationship, even when it affects the other person, you are being selfish. This can lead to controlling behavior as well. Controlling relationships are unhealthy and harmful because you feel the need to exert control over your partner's life in addition to controlling what you do as a pair. You direct them, directing everything from how the dishwasher is loaded to how the bed pillows are inflated: "Do this, not that."

Every connection requires closeness. Without it, the relationship might not work out. Lack of intimacy can be caused by a variety of factors, including not feeling emotionally connected to your partner or not spending enough time together. Intimacy issues frequently cause partners to feel emotionally abandoned and lose interest in having sex, which results in inhibited sexual desire. Couples who dread intimacy may become emotionally distant from one another and engage in a never-ending cycle of limited periods of closeness followed by longer and longer periods of distance.

There is a lot of misunderstanding regarding intimacy, including what it is and how to get it. There are long-married couples who are physically close but lack the emotional intimacy necessary for a healthy relationship. Intimacy needs trust and safety for you to feel free to let go and be who you are. You must be conscious of your inner experience in the present and possess the bravery and flexibility to express what you're experiencing to someone who likewise experiences intimate feelings.

True intimacy requires a genuine level of authenticity that involves being honest in the moment. It's not about talking about your past or your troubles, but rather offering up your feelings about yourself, what's going on in your life right then, or the person you're with. It has a strong sense of immediacy. Understand that your judgments and thoughts are not mere feelings. It takes presence and awareness to connect with true, honest feelings in the present.

To feel confident about yourself and be able to be yourself without worrying about being rejected or judged, you must have self-esteem. If not sincere, stating "I love you" can be less intimate than saying "I don't love you." Sugarcoating the truth prevents you from experiencing the wonderful intimacy that comes with communicating in truth and love. It takes grit, especially when you say something that can make the other person uncomfortable and vice versa.

Every relationship needs to have clear and concise communication. This will help in fending off selfishness and improve intimacy. They might not be able to comprehend each other's wants and expectations if neither spouse can communicate clearly. This could result in misunderstandings and arguments, which might ruin the relationship. To build a solid and healthy bond in a relationship, communication must be unambiguous.

Active listening and honest, open communication are two ways to effectively communicate. This implies that both spouses should try to hear and comprehend each other's opinions and feelings. Additionally, it's crucial to guarantee that expectations are understood and upheld. You can achieve this by being clear about your needs and wants, establishing boundaries, and finding polite solutions to problems.

TOXIC PEOPLE

> "Some people create their storms and then get mad when it rains."
>
> **—Unknown**

It's challenging to get through life without encountering poisonous people. Unfortunately, I've encountered these people many times throughout my life. I've known toxic friends, family, coworkers, and even acquaintances.

These individuals have had a significant impact on my life, making it challenging for me to manage relationships and establish a wholesome atmosphere for myself. The poisonous individual who is perpetually negative is the most prevalent type. They are the ones who are ready to condemn, criticize, and denigrate other people at every turn. They are the ones who are unwilling to accept accountability for their own choices or the results of their words and deeds. They are the ones that will constantly point out something incorrect in any circumstance.

The second type of toxic person is the one who is manipulative and controlling. They're the ones who will try to get their way through any means necessary. They'll use guilt, fear, and intimidation to get people to comply with their wishes. They'll also make sure to make themselves appear to be a victim in every situation, even if they're the cause of the problem.

Then there are the passive-aggressive people. They'll act like everything is fine but then make snide remarks or undermine people behind their backs. They'll also use sarcasm and put-downs to try to make people feel bad about themselves. These types of people have been a part of my life for far too long. I've had to learn how to cope with them and protect myself from their damaging behavior. I've had to work hard to maintain healthy boundaries and relationships with these people and to remind myself that I don't have to put up with their toxic behavior. It's not always easy, but it's worth it in the long run.

How do you deal with these types of people? First, establish boundaries—sound familiar? Set clear boundaries with the person and make sure they are aware of them. Keep yourself safe at the same time you're setting boundaries. If the person is physically or emotionally dangerous, make sure to keep yourself and others out of harm's way. So you're not sucked into their drama, don't engage them, and especially don't engage in arguments with them. Don't take it personally. This part is super hard to do because toxic people are often projecting their insecurities and frustrations onto you. Don't make excuses for them. Don't excuse their negative behavior or try to rationalize it because you are only enabling their toxicity. Seek support and reach out to supportive friends and family members for emotional support. If the situation is beyond your control, seek professional help.

There are three types of toxic personalities you need to be on the lookout for: the victim, the rescuer, and the persecutor. The victim is always looking for someone to help them, and they hold others responsible for their problems. To control others and win their sympathy, they frequently adopt the victim persona. The rescuer is a personality always prepared to "rescue" the sufferer by assuming responsibility for their issues and providing answers. They frequently exhibit codependence and are willing to sacrifice their wants to make the victim happy. The persecutor personality type is always pointing out other people's shortcomings and attempting to make them feel guilty or embarrassed of their deeds. They frequently pass judgment, criticize, and abuse their position of authority to manipulate or dominate people.

A toxic person defies reason. Some people seem blissfully unconscious of the harm they cause to those around them, while others seem to find pleasure in causing commotion and setting off other people. They add needless complexity, conflict, and—worst of all—stress in either case.

Stress has a long history of having detrimental, long-lasting effects on the brain, according to studies. The neurons in the hippocampus, a crucial part of the brain in charge of reasoning and memory, become less effective after being exposed to stress for even a short period of time. Neuronal dendrites—the tiny "arms" that brain cells use to communicate with one another—are damaged by stress after a few weeks and can be permanently destroyed after a few months. Stress is a formidable threat to your success—when stress gets out of control, your brain and your performance suffer.

Your performance directly correlates with your capacity to control your emotions and maintain composure under pressure. More than a million people participated in research that showed that 90 percent of top performers are adept at controlling their emotions under pressure to remain composed and in charge. Their capacity to remove troublesome individuals from their sphere of influence is one of their greatest talents.

Top performers have developed coping mechanisms that they use to avoid harmful people, such as setting limits on exposure to these people and distancing when those limits have been reached. They pick their battles. Sometimes it's better to walk away and "lose" a fight than to metaphorically die on some proverbial hill not worth dying on. And last, they rise above the irrational, often sensationalist, behavior of toxic people, stay away from negative emotions, and keep moving forward with their lives.

This can often be easier said than done. That's why sometimes the only way to get away from toxicity is to just cut it out of your life altogether. This can be hard when it's a close friend or even a family member and even more difficult when that individual is part of your support network, especially if that network is limited. But, again, it's better to live to fight another day, right?

CHAPTER 8
PLEASURE AND HAPPINESS

> *Never regret anything that made you smile.*
>
> —Mark Twain

When we philosophically analyze the concept of happiness, we scrutinize the notion of pleasure as immoral. And although pleasure can be purely self-gratifying, it is unfair to dissect pleasure always as a negative. Epicureanism was a Greek philosophy that believed pleasure was the chief good and, thus, the road to happiness. However, these Epicureans, while they were somewhat of the sex, drugs, and rock-and-roll groupies of the ancient world, felt happiness should be derived more from pleasures of the mind than physical pleasure.

I would argue these bygone beatniks developed a philosophy that often contradicted itself because they discouraged lust for power or fame but also looked more favorably on recreational sex, believing that deep love and intimacy were a weakness. On those grounds, they rejected the institution of marriage.

They believed that things that lessen emotional pain would thereby increase a person's happiness. Epicureans further scorned a notion of the afterlife while curiously also teaching not to fear death. So, eat, drink, and be merry, for tomorrow we die!

Just for the record, I'm not implying that any of that is bad. Good and bad are values people apply to concepts. It should be argued, though, that thousands of years of experience have shown that living by pleasure alone, or at least self-serving, individualistic, and materialist pleasures alone, will not lead to long-term happiness. But the Stoics also did not believe in taking vows of poverty, chastity, or silence like some medieval monk. Living modestly might be virtuous living, but starving yourself out in the rain on the street corner is counterproductive to trying to live a flourishing life, too.

Pleasure contributes to happiness as much as happiness deepens our feelings toward pleasure, but the two can be mutually exclusive. For example, having a cold beer after a long day can be pleasurable but not necessarily make you happy or content. It may just be a distraction from that long, miserable day. The same goes for sex. The act of sex itself is very pleasurable (I doubt too many people would disagree), but if the deed is done to just be a temporary comfort or to forget about some negative emotion, then the unhappiness will still be waiting for you after the coital act is over. The pleasurable deed then invokes a sense of guilt instead of contentment. You can also have a moment of happiness that is not associated with pleasure at all but still summons that sense of satisfaction.

Looking back on what I discussed about Aristotle's version of happiness and that eudaemonia comes with activity or action, Aristotle saw pleasure as activity without hindrance. To him, pleasure was neither good nor bad but had a positive connotation if it lent itself to your happiness. However, before you think, *Well, sex, drugs, and rock and roll are pleasurable, and since those things lend to my happiness, Aristotle is okay with that behavior, and I should be too,* you need to realize that Aristotle also viewed pleasure as something that is not at all self-serving. Destroying brain cells via heavy use of mind-altering substances, putting yourself at risk of sexually transmitting infections, damaging your mental state with short-term, emotionally damaging physical relationships, or losing your hearing after hundreds of sessions of high-decibel musical activities can arguably be said to not be self-serving. They are fun and have short-term pleasures, but in the name of the long game, do they lead to a deep state of happiness?

A neuroscientist will tell you that happiness is nothing more than chemical and electrical processes in the human brain. Just primal catalysts such as motivation and reward. If I am hungry, then I hunt for food. When I get the food, I am happy. I am no neuroscientist, but I would argue that this definition is an oversimplification of the level of happiness we are trying to achieve. What these people who are much smarter than me are telling you is the effects of dopamine. Dopamine is a chemical neurotransmitter that the human nervous system uses to provide that reward we just mentioned. If I find food, I get a shot of dopamine, and I feel a temporary level of pleasure. Anything pleasurable can trigger dopamine: food, sex, alcohol, drugs, likes on social media, exercise, or whatever you find satisfying. So, the very thing that drove us to survive is being used to feed our addictions. This does not lead to happiness—it is the very opposite.

> "Continuous pleasure ceases to be a pleasure."
>
> —Voltaire

Pleasure is a good thing. I think we can all agree there. It feeds your happiness and can aid your journey to eudaemonia. A cold, smooth drink, the warm and erotic embrace of a lover, and fresh chocolate chip cookies straight out of Mom's oven all can lead to a high level of pleasure. However, it must be practiced in moderation with healthy pleasures like good relationships, exercise, healthy eating, continuous personal learning, and growth. Otherwise, you become nothing but a hedonist walking close to an emotional edge where a far fall could have dire consequences for your mind, body, and soul.

HAPPINESS NOT HEDONISM

> "You can live to be a hundred if you give up all the things that make you want to live to be a hundred."
>
> —Woody Allen

Epicurus (341–270 BCE) was another Ancient Greek philosopher who founded a highly influential school of thought named after himself. Epicureanism was founded five years before Zeno of Citium established Stoa to achieve the same goal as Stoicism—to find happiness and tranquility.

The difference is that Epicurus's thought process, as mentioned before, was that happiness came from pursuing pleasure, within moderation, and avoiding those things that cause pain. This aligned with an even older train of thought that pleasure equaled good and pain equaled evil. This is a paradoxical paradigm that happiness *is* pleasure. When pleasure is equated to happiness, then hedonism arises. However, when the point to your happiness is physical pleasure alone, then frustration will soon set in because physical pleasure is a finite feeling. When the feeling wears off, when the dopamine fix is gone, then you don't feel happy anymore because the sensation of what you are equating to satisfaction is no longer there.

I think it fair to point out that the modern definition of hedonism is somewhat different from its origins. Hedonism was a Greek school of philosophy that was remarkably simple: anything that affects you positively is a pleasure, and pleasure is good; anything that affects you negatively is a pain, and pain is bad. Now, we can easily poke holes in that level of thinking.

I mean, drinking all night with your pals makes you feel good, but the next day, the resulting hangover makes you feel bad. So, was the partying good overall or just good until your head started pounding in the morning as you laid yourself out as a sacrifice to the porcelain god? I'm sure doing a line of cocaine brings pleasure at the time, but if you die because of overdosing, was it that good for you? Probably not.

Hedonism's modern description is more puritanical, tending to make the yearning for pleasure immoral. This is, of course, because we limit the definition of pleasure to just a small group of activities like sex, drugs, drinking, partying, etc. The Hedonists of old didn't hamstring themselves in such a way. Food pleases us, but too much can lead to gluttony and a myriad of health issues we covered in Section One.

Sleep pleases us, but staying in bed too long can lead to being slothful or lazy. Hedonists, much like their Epicurean and Stoic brethren, believed in balance. The proverbial scales needed to be in balance between pleasure and being in agony all the time—physically, mentally, spiritually, or otherwise.

> "Many a man thinks he is buying pleasure, when he is really selling himself to it."
> —Benjamin Franklin

The famous quote by Benjamin Franklin about man's relationship with pleasure is a thought-provoking reminder of the dangers of addiction. It speaks to the idea that when a person is trying to find pleasure in activities or substances, they may be doing more harm than good.

When you are in pursuit of pleasure, you may be unaware of the consequences of your actions. Pleasure is often seen as a reward, and you may think that by engaging in pleasurable activities or using substances, you can make yourself feel better. However, what you may not realize is that you are selling yourself short in the process.

When you are dependent on substances or activities to make you feel good, you are limiting the potential to achieve true happiness. The notion of selling oneself for pleasure is a slippery slope. When pleasure is sought in activities or substances, the risk of addiction increases. Addiction is a powerful force, and it can take over a person's life if they are not careful. Instead of achieving pleasure, addiction can lead to problems such as financial ruin, strained relationships, and health issues.

Pleasure can be a healthy part of life, but it should not be pursued in excess. Instead of "buying" pleasure, you should focus on cultivating meaningful relationships, engaging in activities that bring joy, and taking care of your physical and mental health. These are the things that lead to true and lasting happiness.

SEX AND HAPPINESS

> "Sex: the thing that takes up the least amount of time and causes the most amount of trouble."
>
> —John Barrymore

Sex is great! I mean, c'mon, am I right? Without getting graphic, a healthy sex life, with emphasis on the word *healthy,* is well-known to increase happiness. Self-help books often leave out the discussion of sex because of various taboos, religious beliefs, and the author's fear of turning away readers.

It's rather a shame that this is the case because it is a subject as old as humanity that is often not discussed openly or maturely. I'm not going to go into detail about whether masturbating four times a day is normal or whether you and your significant other should role-play once a month to spice up your sex life. That's between you and your significant other, and perhaps a good therapist, but sex is still a normal part of the human experience and, much like any pleasurable thing, can cause a full spectrum of both positive and negative emotions.

Sex can be healthy or unhealthy, and throughout history, it has been used as a tool, a gift, and as a weapon. Ultimately, sex is the sole reason mankind continues to exist on planet Earth. Sex and happiness are two concepts that are deeply intertwined in our modern society. From the time we are born, we are taught that having a healthy sex life is a major factor in achieving true happiness. This is because sex is seen to express love and affection, as well as physical pleasure. Sexual pleasure is one of the most powerful forms of physical pleasure, and as a result, it has been linked to feelings of happiness and contentment.

The relationship between sex and happiness is complex and can be affected by many factors. For example, the quality of the relationship you have with your partner, the amount of communication within the relationship, and the satisfaction of both partners can all play a part in how happy you feel when it comes to sex. Additionally, the type of sex you are engaging in can have a major impact on the level of happiness you experience. For example, if you are engaging in sex that is solely focused on physical pleasure and not emotional connection, then it is unlikely to lead to happiness.

Moreover, research has shown that having a regular sex life can lead to increased levels of happiness. This is because sexual activity releases chemicals in the brain that are linked to feelings of pleasure and happiness. Regular sex can also lead to improved relationships. There is a lot of science behind sex.

Many university researchers have done study after study to not only determine the physical aspects of sex but also the mental and emotional facets and how the act of lovemaking increases positivity. Plenty of evidence exists to show that sex does make you happier. The University of Toronto-Mississauga studied heterosexual couples in committed relationships between the ages of eighteen and eighty-nine and found that there was a correlation between the frequency of physical intimacy and happiness. The University of Chicago continually conducts a biannual survey looking at similar data and consistently finds the same results. However, both studies have a "gotcha" in the data. Apparently, *more* isn't always *better*. The sweet spot is only having sex once a week.

Hang with me for a minute! Just keep reading; it'll all make sense.

The typical stereotypes of men having a higher libido than women and that the older someone gets, the less sex they have were proven to not change the unswerving results of the various studies. Despite age, race, gender, sexuality, and marital status, the data led to the same outcome: people who have sex once a week are the happiest.

There are some of you greatly disappointed now and others rejoicing. Sorry, folks, data doesn't lie.

Carnegie-Mellon University found that the reason happiness decreased with frequency was because when couples were told that they *had to have sex* for the sake of the study, it was no longer about physical intimacy, emotional closeness, or love but more of just a physical act with no substance. Sex must have a sense of *meaning* for the act to create longer-lasting happiness instead of just a quick dopamine fix.

You have physical needs, yes, and that often is interpreted as a *need* for sex. But it's not really about sex. No. You want intimacy and the connection between people that comes from intimacy. You need to be touched physically, to be admired, to be emotionally attached. You want someone to smile at you, ask how your day went, and yearn to know your needs, desires, and dreams. You want a genuinely safe space with another human being where you can laugh and cry and even vent on your bad days. That's what you sincerely crave. The exchange of bodily fluids after flesh-to-flesh friction and, hopefully, the orgasmic release at the end is just a bonus.

LUST

> "Lust is a thing of blood. Doesn't need head nor heart."
>
> —Karen Marie Moning

Lust is a funny thing. It can be the most powerful, intoxicating feeling in the world, and at the same time, it can be incredibly fleeting and easy to lose sight of. Lust is the physiological force that creates an intense sexual desire for another person. The philosophical realm of sex is that it is an expression of love and unity.

The Bible says, "They shall become one flesh," an allusion to the very act of sex where the two lovers are physically connected. Erotic passion, in such regards, is about consuming another into yourself, mind, body, and soul, whether the result is physical, emotional, or both. Healthy passion is between two consenting adults who are in a committed relationship and looking to have both their physical and emotional needs met but are consuming for the sake of the other. It is selfless. But lust, the very desire to sexually consume another, left to its own devices, will never stop wanting to consume until it consumes the luster. And it's a lot more than just a physical thing.

Lust is the feeling you get when you're looking at someone, and you want them to know how much they mean to you, even if they don't know yet. It's the feeling of wanting to be with them, even if it means sacrificing other things in your life—like maybe a relationship or schoolwork or friends or family. Legend says that lust caused Queen Guinevere to cheat on King Arthur with his most favored knight, Sir Lancelot, an act that eventually led to the very fall of Camelot and Arthur's demise, which was ironic seeing that according to one version of the story, Arthur himself was conceived out of an act of lust and infidelity when his father, Uther, disguised himself as another man and slept with the man's unknowing wife.

Lust is a complicated thing. It's both an emotion and a sensation. It can be pleasurable and painful. And it's often confused with love. But when you look at what lust really is all about, you'll see that it's not just another emotion—it's a perspective. This hunger is what drives us to explore new things, seek out new experiences, or pursue someone we love even harder than we did before. Lust can make you feel alive, make you feel like you belong somewhere in the world.

Lust is the fuel that keeps our hearts beating and our bodies moving—and without it, we'd probably just sit around all day doing nothing but watching TV. Lust is also a dangerous thing. It's like a drug, and it makes you want to do things you wouldn't normally do—things that could get you in trouble.

Lust can take over your life, and you'll spend all your time thinking about sex and what sex would be like if only you had the right partner. You'll wonder whether it's worth it to have sex with him or her because of all the work that will follow: planning, cleaning up after, and using protection. Moral values tell you that you're not supposed to feel this way about someone who isn't your partner! But lust just makes us do it anyway. And if we don't do anything about it, then we're going to end up doing something that isn't good for us or our relationships.

So, when you're feeling lusty, but you don't know where to start—or maybe you just haven't figured out how to turn your lust into something more satisfying than just some random hookup—here are a few things to consider: sex is the most widely used recreational activity in the world. Humans have a primordial impulse to seek pleasure, and this urge is one of our strongest motivators.

What if you were able to transcend the material? What if you were able to have sexual experiences when your mind and body are intertwined? More than simply physical pleasure is involved in sex. It also entails feeling an emotional connection to someone else. Because of this, I think that having sex should be more than just a physical act; it should also be a chance to get to know your spouse or partner better.

Sex is a way of connecting with someone that goes beyond all other forms of connection. It allows people to express their delight and sorrow, happiness, and unhappiness. And when you're connected in that sense, you can't help but feel joyful because you know that you have each other, no matter what happens in the outside world.

Being physically close to someone is only one aspect of sex; it also involves developing a spiritual connection with them. Sexual intimacy makes you a part of the other person, sharing their emotions and ideas. During sex, your partner is viewing themselves through your eyes when they speak to you or look at you, and the reverse is also true. Because of how strongly sex binds us together, we frequently overlook the fact that we also require emotional closeness from one another in addition to physical intimacy.

Having said all of this, I'll point out that one of the most pervasive misconceptions about lust is that it's exclusively sexual. However, lust can also be about other things, such as a sense of love or connection for another person. Lust can even be connected to feelings of safety and security; if you experience lust when there is no immediate risk, this indicates that your brain is telling you there isn't one around. Because lust comes from our brains rather than our bodies, it can happen at any time and in any situation—even when we're not looking for something specific or ready to act on our feelings.

PORNOGRAPHY PROBLEM

> "Sports is to war as pornography is to sex."
> **—Jonathan Haidt**

Sex *is not* pornography. Yes, pornography is the visualization of the act of sex. I mean, the actors are having sex in the scene being filmed, but what I'm talking about is the real version of human intercourse and not what is being misrepresented in a grungy studio. This is the problem with pornography when it comes to happiness.

Pornography has been proven to lead to discontentment, unhealthy relationships, and addiction. Further analysis has shown that porn watching has led to a loss of sexual pleasure in both men and women and even erectile dysfunction. Studies of young men who became addicted to pornography spent vast amounts of money that they didn't have to subscribe to porn sites, neglected their studies and their jobs, and became isolated from friends and family. Sounds like every other addiction, right? Similar characteristics are found in alcoholics, junkies, and gambling addicts. All of this leads to depression as well as other antisocial behaviors that aren't healthy for the addict or those around them.

Further, and much more disturbing, these studies found that porn addicts became controlling in their relationships, had increased anxiety levels, and became narcissistic. All of this coupled with low self-esteem and depression creates an unhealthy, introverted person. To get to the point, it's a dark hole of unhappiness, which isn't the goal of what we're trying to get to.

And it gets worse.

I know this sounds like a college thesis paper but bear with me on this because it is important. Addictive fixations rewire the human brain, and the more exposure to the addiction, the more neural pathways are created to facilitate the dependence, in this case, on pornographic imagery. (Neural pathways are connections throughout the brain and nervous system that allow the brain to talk to the body.) Soon those pathways become more and more automatic, and this defines a male's interaction with females. Warped and sometimes demented perceptions of how women should be treated are formed. Women are objectified as elements of pleasure alone, and false impressions of beauty and dignity become normalized in the addict's mind.

While porn is vastly diverse to meet the liking of the addict, it still paints the picture of the skinny, big-boobed female who is willing and able to do anything inherently sexual. It often shows heavy-set or small-breasted women to be fetishes versus mainstream. I won't even get into what all is wrong with Anime pornography. (I'll give you a hint: tentacles!) Despite what some porn advocates may tell you, none of this is empowering to women and only leads to further fractures in a civilized society already beaten to hell by other problems.

> "There is no dignity when the human dimension is eliminated from the person. In short, the problem isn't that pornography shows too much of the person, but that it shows far too little."
>
> —Pope John Paul II

Pornography misinterprets how the act of sex itself should be experienced. I mean, if you are a gymnast and can flex that much for that long, hell, more power to you, dear reader. It is a deeply concerning fact that porn itself is extremely demeaning to women. Depicting women as always promiscuous, easy, and willing to commit to any sexual act, including acts of violence and depravity.

Grammy-award-winning American singer Billie Eilish admitted in 2021 interviews that watching pornography at an early age, eleven years old, greatly impacted her mental state. She saw violent and rough acts performed by the actresses and associated them with how sexual intercourse was supposed to be. She said, "The first few times I, you know, had sex, I was not saying no to things that were not good. It was because I thought that's what I was supposed to be attracted to."

Porn also paints an unrealistic portrait of masculinity and what men *should* look like. Porn makes men feel inferior if they're not hung like a horse, as the actors in the films are portrayed. When a person feels inadequate due to what he sees in porn, then porn just becomes the alternative to seeking out healthy relationships, regardless of the person's sexuality.

I know I'm getting ahead of another chapter, but here is a very important truth you need to grasp: there is no real intimacy in pornography—no love, no comfort, no commitment, nada. If you haven't been paying attention, emotional love is one of the three things we *need* to be happy, and porn instead sensationalizes the physical act of love but divorces the genuine emotional and psychological pleasure that sex derives from the very relationship that it is in.

Casual sex, "booty calls," and one-night stands all have severely negative effects on the human psyche—for both men and women. When people get older, these effects are like tearing holes in a window screen, where unwanted creepy crawlies can start to get in. It's annoying at first, but then moths start filling up your lampshades, and spiders start crawling in your ears at night. The truth is that physical sex and emotional love are inherently interconnected, always have been, and always will be, so don't let Hollywood lie to you.

Much like others suffering from addiction, the porn addict becomes increasingly curious, trying to find the images that create more dopamine hits in the brain as he or she becomes numb to what they are already viewing. I probably don't have to tell you that there is some dark, twisted shit on the internet, and much like the alcoholic drinking more because he or she has built a higher tolerance, so will the porn addict. And while they are an amazing stress reliever, orgasms are believed to be short-term cures for headaches. Porn is not about stress relief or even short-term pleasures.

Understand that the act of lovemaking should not be ruled by egos or lustful desires. It is an act of intimacy, a period of vulnerability, an epoch of trust between individuals that brings a deeper sense of happiness and contentment. It is sacred, or at least it should be. Sex is more than procreation, and while that alone is also sacrosanct, to just be about carrying on lineage or population takes away from one of the grand reasons humans make love in the first place and not just to have sex to get pregnant like the animal population.

It's so we do not feel so alone.

Porn not only prevents healthy relationships but can annihilate them. Studies on pornography further prove that married couples who start watching porn, even together, have double the chance of separation and or divorce. While men tend to take the heaviest hit on the "porn is bad" scale, women are just as affected and three times as likely to leave a relationship because of their viewing habits!

I'm not a therapist in any shape or form, but if you are struggling with porn addiction, the first thing to do is admit it. Admit it to yourself, your spouse, partner, or significant other, and then—together—seek professional help before you do irreparable harm to your relationship, your psyche, and your happiness.

HEALTHY SEX AND HAPPINESS

> "Good sex begins when your clothes are still on."
> —W. Masters & V. Johnson

I know we have gone down the negative side of sex, but if sex is just used as a temporary fix to supplant some deeper hurt or discouragement, like when "sex is just sex," it becomes no better than drugs or alcohol. When sex is just to get a dopamine hit, then it is cheapened; the sacrosanct viscosity of the very act is diluted so much that it fails to carry any kind of lubrication to the ball bearings of the soul.

We use apps on smartphones to conjure up a booty call like we would a hamburger at a fast-food restaurant and think nothing of it because we think we're just giving society the middle finger. I don't care what society thinks, but I bet our hearts and minds do. Society doesn't make us happy. Oh, and by the way, it never will. Our self-esteem and strength of consciousness do, however. If sex is just a placeholder for something we are missing, then we will never find what we are looking for and will forever be lost in the abyss of unhappiness. This starts with communication with our spouse, partner, or significant other.

Healthy sexual behavior goes beyond the physical. It's about being in a committed partnership, enjoying life to the fullest, and being confident in who you are. It is figuring out how to make your partner feel important in your life despite everything else that is going on. And it's about taking care of oneself, whether that entails scheduling time for exercise or getting adequate sleep. Although having sex may be the last thing from your thoughts when under stress, it's crucial to keep in mind that having sex can improve your physical and emotional well-being.

Sex is integral to a healthy relationship. It's been scientifically proven that having sex regularly helps with everything from staying fit to improving your mood, lowering your stress level, and even preventing illness. Now that's better than chewable vitamin C!

Occasionally, we all struggle with the concept of sex and how to ensure that it is enjoyable for both partners. Simple things like making sure your nails are trimmed or simply being open to trying new things are just a couple of the many things you can do to ensure you're providing your partner the finest experience possible. It's a beautiful thing, and it can be an amazing source of pleasure. But sex has so much more to offer than just a good time; it's an opportunity for connection and intimacy, for experience and learning, for growth and healing. And when you're having sex the right way—when you're doing it in positive alignment with your own needs, desires, and boundaries—you'll find that sex helps you reach your goals.

You'll feel more capable, more confident, happier at work and in your relationships, and ultimately more fulfilled as a person! Healthy sex can be hard to come by because it requires effort and trust from both people involved. But once you have those things in place, the benefits are endless: more intimacy, enhanced communication, better sex . . . the list goes on. And once you start feeling those things, you find yourself a happier, more content person living inside your eudaemonia.

UNHEALTHY PRACTICES

> "Kinky is using a feather. Perverted is using the whole chicken."
>
> —Unknown

There are plenty of stories written throughout history that are put on a pedestal as the very essence of romance when the behavior is unhealthy and destructive.

The legend of King Arthur is well proliferated on how Arthur's wife, Guinevere, has an ongoing affair with Sir Lancelot, a Knight of the Round Table and Arthur's lieutenant. If you dig into the various levels of storytelling and poetry written about the affair, you will see that the two fall in love after Lancelot saves Guinevere from a kidnapping. They're infatuated with one another, and it could easily be sewn into the fabric of the literature that the taboo of the forbidden relationship makes it exciting for the two, as with most affairs. The result, however, is more than just a celebrity marriage falling apart; it leads to chaos within King Arthur's court. This ultimately opens the door to enemies of Camelot usurping the kingdom, King Arthur's death in battle, and the destruction of Camelot itself. Some poetry goes on to tell how both Guinevere and Lancelot go on to live the rest of their lives in monasteries, alone and shunned.

Often, within the excitement of the moment, such a travesty is often disregarded or considered *worth the risk*, and while it may not beget the downfall of kingdoms, infidelity has destroyed families and demolished happiness.

Now, I'm not here to judge anyone on their lifestyles or the choices they make in life. Everyone has a reason why they do the things they do. The message I write about is that there are certain behaviors that go against the journey of being happy, content, and prosperous, and often the things that make us happy now, those fleeting pleasures, only lead to the pain our Hedonist ancestors believed in.

Adultery is a state of being unfaithful to your spouse. It's cheating, plain and simple. And it's significant. Adultery is more than just having sex with someone else; it also implies that you don't value your relationship with your partner. Not only do you want to be with someone else, but you also want to replace your partner.

Adultery deprives you of the love and intimacy you may have with your spouse and is a severe type of selfishness. Adultery violates your marriage vows, destroys trust, and causes great harm to the individual who believes they should be your spouse. There are numerous potential outcomes if you commit adultery, including divorce, loss of child custody or visitation rights, loss of support from friends, and guilty feelings that may persist for years after the fact.

The subject of polygamy is contentious. Although it has been practiced for centuries, we have only just started to think about the potential negative effects. A system of marriage known as polygamy involves a man having numerous wives and spouses. Although it was once accepted as the norm, it is now prohibited in many nations. Even in the United States, specifically in the state of Utah, polygamy was not officially illegal until 2015.

One in five US individuals who were unmarried at the time of a 2016 poll and who participated in that poll had previously been in a consensually non-monogamous relationship. A year later, a Canadian poll published approximately the same results. According to Justin Lehmiller, social psychologist and research fellow at the Kinsey Institute for Research in Sex, Gender, and Reproduction in Bloomington, Indiana, "Another thing we've seen in the last decade is that Google searches for the terms *polyamorous* and *open relationship* have increased, which demonstrates that there's more interest in this topic." But Lehmiller notes that individuals who have been involved in these kinds of interactions have been going on for a long time and are really nothing new, except now, in the twenty-first century, these relationships are becoming more overt.

Polyamorous relationships, while they can be fulfilling and beneficial for those involved, can also present unique challenges and risks. As with any relationship, communication is key to maintaining a healthy, successful relationship, and this is especially true for polyamorous relationships. There are a few key dangers that can arise, and it is important to be aware of them to ensure that all parties involved are safe and happy.

The first danger that can arise from polyamorous relationships is the risk of jealousy. When two or more people are involved in a relationship, there is a greater chance of jealousy becoming an issue, as each person may feel as though they are not getting enough attention or care from their partner. This can lead to feelings of insecurity and resentment and, if not addressed and resolved, can cause serious harm to the relationship. It is important to be open and honest with your partners and to communicate any feelings of jealousy that come up.

The risk of hurt feelings is also increased when multiple people are in a relationship, as they become emotionally invested in each other. This can lead to hurt feelings if one partner does something that another finds unacceptable. This could range from a partner not showing enough attention to one person to one partner sleeping with another partner without the third partner's knowledge. It is important to talk openly and honestly with all partners involved to ensure that everyone's feelings are respected and taken into consideration.

The third danger that can arise from polyamorous relationships is the risk of sexually transmitted diseases (STDs). As with any sexual relationship, it is important to practice safe sex and to use contraception to prevent the spread of STDs. It is important to talk openly and honestly with all partners about their sexual health and to ensure that everyone is on the same page about safe sex practices.

Communication is key, and it is important to talk openly and honestly with all partners to ensure that everyone's feelings are respected and taken into consideration. Less than 1 percent of married persons are in open or polyamorous relationships, according to Steve Brody, PhD, a psychotherapist in Cambria, California. According to certain studies, open or polyamorous relationships fail 92 percent of the time. Open or polyamorous marriages are thus even more rare, and they also have a 92 percent chance of ending in divorce.

> "Stop setting yourself on fire for people who just want to watch you burn."
> —Nadège Richards

The swinging lifestyle is a way of life that emphasizes liberty, autonomy, and physical enjoyment. Sexual activity occurs outside the bounds of a relationship, either by one partner or as a couple, but with the knowledge of both partners. It is different than a polyamorous relationship because the sex is considered recreational, and the overall commitment remains between the original partners. While it can be a fun and pleasurable activity for some couples, it also carries with it some risks that should be considered before engaging in it.

The first risk associated with the swinging lifestyle is the risk of sexually transmitted diseases, including HIV. Swingers may be engaging in unprotected sexual activities with multiple partners, putting themselves and their partners at risk of contracting an STD. While many swingers are aware of the risks and take precautions to protect themselves and their partners, there is still the possibility of an STD being transmitted. Therefore, if you are considering engaging in the swinging lifestyle, it is important to practice safe sex and use protection whenever possible.

From 2007 to 2008, three sexual health clinics in South Limburg, the Netherlands, which provide care to a population of 630,000, routinely recorded if a patient was a swinger to track the infection rates in this community. There were a little under 9,000 consultations at the three clinics over the research period. Swingers made up one in nine patients (12 percent).

Swingers, young individuals, and homosexual men—groups recognized as being at high risk—had the greatest incidence of sexually transmitted diseases in this study. The rates of chlamydia and gonorrhea combined were a little over 10 percent among straight persons, 14 percent among homosexual males, under 5 percent among prostitutes, and 10.4 percent among swingers. Compared to male swingers, female swingers had greater infection rates.

One in seven patients at these clinics were between the ages of thirty-five and forty-five, and one in nine (11.7 percent) were above the age of forty-five. Swingers received more than half (55 percent) of all diagnoses in the over-forty-five age group compared to gay males, who received around a third (31 percent) of diagnoses. Around one in ten (10 percent) older swingers had chlamydia, and one in twenty (5 percent), had gonorrhea.

Another risk associated with the swinging lifestyle is the risk of emotional and psychological harm. It is important to remember that swinging is a sexual activity and can be emotionally and psychologically draining for some individuals. This is especially true for people who are not used to the lifestyle and who may not be emotionally or psychologically prepared for the emotions and feelings that can come up when engaging in this type of activity. It is important to make sure that both partners are comfortable and willing to engage in the activity before participating.

Finally, the swinging lifestyle can also lead to conflict between partners. Since partners are engaging in sexual activities with multiple people, jealousy and insecurity may arise. This can lead to arguments and even breakups if the couple is not prepared to handle the emotions that may arise.

> "If God's got anything better than sex to offer, he's certainly keeping it to himself."
>
> —Sting

I know I've whacked you in the face with a few pages of some of the negativity surrounding sex, but have no fear—sex is still a good thing. It's a great thing if it's safe and in a place of trust and happiness. I'll reiterate the statement from before: many of us think that intimacy is just about sex, but we could not be further from reality. Intimacy—real intimacy—is about reciprocating truth. When your relationship grows to the point where you can tell the truth risk-free from judgment or absolute consequence (such as divorce or death) and show your true self free from any misunderstanding, then both you and your partner will find safety and security, which is a gateway to intimacy. And real intimacy equals happiness.

CHAPTER 9
LOVE AND HAPPINESS

> *Love creates an avenue for happiness to flourish.*
>
> —Unknown

As mentioned many times before, no one can always be happy, but the journey needs to be taken anyway. As social creatures, humans require the various relationships we have with other humans to find that sense of contentment with family, friends, and intimate partners. In other words, we need to be loved.

Love is not a primary relationship specific to an individual or even a group of individuals. Love is an attitude that transcends any single person or thing. True love, not the kind in fairy tales where the prince saves the princess, and they live happily ever after—that's bullshit. But *real*, true love is flawless, resilient, and the purest emotion known to mankind. But to get to that point, it has to be refined like steel, matured like wine, and embraced like an ancient relic discovered from a primeval ruin.

The Greeks had eight separate words for the various forms of human love. For example, *Eros* is physical passion, lust, and love for the sake of physical pleasure. This is where we get the word *erotic* from. Another is *Philia* or brotherly love, hence why Philadelphia is called "the city of brotherly love." It is not a term meaning love between siblings but rather a love between comrades or close compatriots, a feeling felt between soldiers on a battlefield or those who have survived tragedy together, sharing in the trauma and grief of the episode.

Agape is considered the highest form of love. It is universal love but, like many Greek words, has an even deeper meaning. *Agape* is the type of love that is selfless, empathetic, void of ego, and not quid pro quo. It is the type of love shown to a society's elders, a stranger, or other people's children. It is described as the very love God has for mankind. Each of these types of love not only comes with its own description but also different levels of intensity. Further, love is more than a feeling or an action; love is the very substance that fills the many voids in our lives.

Love is the last piece of the happiness puzzle. Like the Foreigner song says, "I want to know what love is." In this case, we need to get down in the weeds and talk about intimate love with our spouses, partners, mates, significant others, pets, etc.

LEVELS OF LOVE

> "Those who fall in love with practice, without science, are like a sailor who enters a ship without a helm or a compass, and who never can be certain whither he is going."
>
> —**Leonardo Da Vinci**

There are three basic stages when it comes to romantic love: desire, passion, and commitment. Desire is the purest form of physical and emotional attraction. It is biochemical, instinctual, and primal, going back to the very first humans to walk the Earth, where there was an automatic and genetic need to reproduce and maintain the species. It is as easy as "Do you want to have sex or not?"

Yet despite its simplicity, the very primitive nature of desire creates irrational thoughts and often unreasonable actions, like teenagers acting on impulse due to the introduction of hormones into their developing bodies. You could tone the term down to infatuation if the word *desire* makes you uncomfortable, but understand, the two are synonymous. It is still the obsessive interest or desire for someone based on their physical attributes.

Desire can be considered an immoral emotion because of the behavior that is often associated with it—sexual acts based solely on physical need, abandoning emotional consideration and rational thought. The persons involved are often devoid of logic in their drive to fulfill the physical want of flesh. Desire leads to acts considered immoral and sinful, such as fornication and adultery. In some cases, especially when referring to the New Testament, the very thought or urge to commit such acts was a sin even without the behavior being acted upon. Greek philosophers took fault with desire because it took away reasonable behavior, as many earlier Western thinkers believed the only thing separating us from animals was our ability to reason and think logically. Therefore, to the philosophers of old, being taken over by such primal instincts was less human.

Desire can be dangerous, less so because of the moral or religious sensitivities associated with it, but because the behavior of desire is often disorganized and directed inappropriately toward the wrong goal. Getting that dopamine hit by getting it on with that stranger after a night of drinking will meet a temporary need but could lead to a variety of, well . . . complications.

Further, it can be dangerous because of how powerful that disorganized direction can be as people essentially allow themselves to be controlled by the impulse and commit acts that have real consequences, like venereal diseases or unexpected pregnancies from unprotected sex, damaged or even destroyed relationships from ignoring the emotional aspects of physical love, and the damaged reputations that come from all of those and similar comportments.

> "You can't blame gravity for falling in love."
> —Albert Einstein

Passion is a more mature form of desire, yet there can still be a level of irrational thought. You could also call it romance if you wanted to. Romance sounds more sensual and idealistic. Nevertheless, the step up from desire is the deeper emotional connection between two people. In other words, we want to have sex not just because our loins are aching but because we want to feel a more profound association with one another. It's what makes us buy flowers or hold boom boxes above our heads playing cheesy 80s music to woo a mate. While passion can be as animalistic as desire, the difference is that passion is intended to lead to more benevolent outcomes, while desire only thirsts for a physical release.

Passion is an essential and fundamental element of a good relationship. It is the spark that ignites and fortifies the bond between two individuals, bringing them closer and more in tune with one another. Physical closeness, spending time together, or simply expressing one's love for the other can all be ways that passion is exhibited.

Couples can quickly drift away if there isn't desire in their relationship since they will feel that something is missing. That spark that keeps a relationship going and developing, passion makes sure that both parties stay interested in and engaged with one another. Couples can have a lifelong, meaningful connection if they are fervent for one another.

> "Love is the commitment to safeguarding another person's heart with the same vigor as you would shield your own."
>
> —Unknown

Commitment is the last level of love. It is what is formed when passion has stuck around long enough to build stronger bonds of trust and mutual respect. It adds serotonin to the dopamine fixes of lust and passion and, after a time, is built around rational thought. Rational thought, as previously mentioned, is the very thing that separates humans from the rest of the animal kingdom.

A strong and fulfilling relationship is built on commitment. It is the cornerstone upon which a solid bond is constructed, and it is crucial that couples learn to rely on and trust one another. Without commitment, relationships can easily deteriorate and end. A committed relationship is one in which both parties are willing to invest the necessary time and effort to make it work. It indicates that both partners are prepared to make concessions and sacrifices when necessary. It also implies that both parties are prepared to try to comprehend one another's needs and desires. Couples that are committed to one another have the assurance that their partner is devoted to them and that their connection is worth maintaining.

Another benefit of commitment is that it enables open and honest communication between partners. It is simpler for a couple to talk about their thoughts and any potential problems when both partners are devoted to the union. This makes it more likely that both parties will comprehend one another and be able to collaborate on a solution.

Couples who are committed to one another can create a solid bond that is based on mutual respect, understanding, and trust. Couples can work together to build a long-lasting relationship that is characterized by love, joy, and fulfillment if they are committed to doing so.

> "You may not be her first, her last, or her only. She loved before; she may love again. But if she loves you now, what else matters?"
> —Bob Marley

You will fall in love with three people in your lifetime, and each one is for a specific and special reason. Your first love happens when you are young. It eventually ends, and you grow apart or break up over immature things. As you age, you look back on those and consider that it wasn't love, but the reality is, it was driven by hormones and a lack of education of what love really is but nevertheless, love.

The second love is the more difficult one because you tend to get hurt more when this one ends. However, it teaches you life lessons and makes you more resilient. This love almost always includes betrayal, lies, abuse, drama, psychological pain, and sometimes physical pain, and as you grow, you realize more and more that the more you learn about love, the less you really know.

The third and last love comes blindly, creeping silently, striking without warning because it comes from a direction you're not looking in. Walls will go up and then get torn down. You let the person in and find yourself caring more and more about them. This isn't the fairytale love we read about in Hans Christian Anderson's stories, but you will still find yourself lost in the other's eyes, your heart palpitating, and your mind getting entrapped thinking of nothing other than being with that person. You see past imperfections and disregard errors, and this often leads to marriage and family.

UNCONDITIONAL LOVE

> "To give and not expect a return, that is what lies at the heart of love."
>
> —Oscar Wilde

A soldier returned to the States after serving in Vietnam. He called his parents from a payphone in San Francisco. "Mom, Dad, I'm coming home. But I have a favor. I'm bringing a friend with me. Is that okay?"

"Of course, "they replied, "we'd be delighted to meet him."

The soldier continued, "That's great, but there is something you need to know. He was wounded in battle. He lost an arm and a leg. He has nowhere to go. No family to return to. I want him to come and live with us."

The mom gasped, "That's terrible, son! Maybe we can help find him a place to live."

The son replied, "No, Mom, I want him to live with us."

The father retorted, "Son, you don't know what you're asking. Someone like that requires a lot of help. Our home isn't built for that. This will be a great burden on our family. Just come home. Let the VA take care of your friend."

The son hung up the phone. The mother and father heard nothing for a long time until the phone rang one day, and it was the San Francisco Police Department calling. Their son had committed suicide, and they were needed to identify and claim the body. The grief-stricken mother and father were distraught. What could have driven him to such an end? They hastened to San Francisco to claim their son, and when they got to the morgue, they were shocked to find that he was missing an arm and a leg.

Okay, I know this was a depressing tale, but the moral of the story is that it is easy to love people when they look good, when they are whole, and when they are not a burden on our lives. Sometimes we'd rather stay away from the ugly, the ill, the maimed, those who do not share our values or our interests. It gets hard to love someone when life isn't easy.

Now, surely if the son in the story had told his parents he had been maimed in the war, or even just showed up at the house in his current condition, they would have loved him regardless. We would assume. Going off the story their son was giving them, it was easy to push away because the "friend" was a stranger, and they had no obligation to support him.

> "Unconditional love is an illogical notion, but such a great and powerful one."
> —A. J. Jacobs

I have read that story dozens of times in my life, all with the same meaning and moral, but it wasn't until I read it with the sole purpose of introducing it to my manuscript that it dawned on me: what made the son feel that he needed to fabricate a story of a wounded friend to see if his parents would accept him? Maybe the son didn't feel loved before he left for war. It's apparent the son didn't feel loved *unconditionally*. Mark Manson, in his book *The Subtle Art of Not Giving A F*ck*, pontificates on this. He says, "Acts of love are valid only if they're performed without conditions or expectations."

> "You know that place between sleep and awake, the place where you can still remember dreaming? That's where I will always love you. That's where I'll be waiting."
>
> —James M. Barrie, *Peter Pan or The Boy Who Wouldn't Grow Up* (1904)

The quote from Peter Pan on this page is one of my favorites. You may find it corny or cliché, but in those words, I find there is patient desperation, quixotic heartbreak, and accepted longing. A feeling so strong that it transcends consciousness and extends into the ether of dream. It's a statement so bold as to be transformational because if it is genuine, then it is eternal. He says, "I will always love you," always implying an absolute. Absolute also means unconditional. The words can fit almost anywhere in a myriad of scenarios, from someone going away on a five-month deployment to someone who just does not know if they'll see the other person again. It's the last line, "That's where I'll be waiting," where I feel unconditional love. No matter the circumstances, the distance, the obstacles, whether that even be death itself—*I will love you, and I will be waiting.* How can you read that and not lose your breath?

Inhale. Hold. Exhale.

How can unconditional love make you happy? Well, if you are receiving unconditional love, that will be obvious. It will make you more satisfied. If you've been paying attention to this chapter, then you know that I have been telling you that *giving* unconditional love to others will make you even happier and even more content than *receiving* that love. (Hint: there will be an internal theme with this subject.) But what makes love *unconditional*? It is love without limitation, without conditions or clauses, without expecting anything in return . . . not even a thank you.

The Greek word for unconditional love is *agape*. If one is going to find some deep meaning in the concept of unconditional love, the Christian Bible is a good place to start.

1Corinthians 13:4 tells us: "Love is patient, love is kind. Love is not jealous, it does not brag, and it is not proud. Love is not rude, is not selfish, and does not get upset with others. Love does not count up wrongs that have been done. Love takes no pleasure in evil but rejoices over the truth. Love patiently accepts all things. It always trusts, always hopes, and always endures. Love never ends."

Much like Aristotle believed that happiness requires activity, the Apostle Paul shows that unconditional love also requires action. You must *be* patient. You must *be* kind. You must *be* trusting. Just sitting on your behind and saying you're all those things is not enough to meet the goal here, folks.

There is longevity to this application as well. Love *always* trusts, *always* endures. Always refers to *all* occasions. Unconditional love doesn't take a break or pick and choose the circumstances in which it will act. Now, this doesn't mean you won't or can't feel certain emotions. It's not a sin to be impatient at times, and being occasionally mean or losing your temper doesn't make you a monster. Trust, as well, is a learned feeling that must be refined and doesn't come easy—and shouldn't, for that matter. That is what makes unconditional love all that more powerful because you overcome those feelings and emotions and come out on the other side with a more beautiful perspective.

In his best-selling book, *Everything is F*cked: A Book About Hope*, the sequel to his *The Subtle Art of Not Giving a F*ck*, Mark Manson wrote that "To transcend the transactional realm of hope, one must act unconditionally. You must love someone without expecting anything in return; otherwise, it's not truly love. You must respect someone without expecting anything in return; otherwise, you don't truly respect him. You must speak honestly without expecting a pat on the back or a high-five or a gold star next to your name; otherwise, you aren't truly being honest." The human condition makes this difficult.

Loving in such a selfless way produces the same chemical response as romantic love. As mentioned before, eudaemonia is much deeper than an ancient genetic carrot-and-stick system. If dopamine alone were enough, we wouldn't have depression or anxiety disorders. Giving and receiving unconditional love creates a strong sense of security and healthy attachments while also fostering autonomy, independence, and a durable level of self-confidence. Unconditional love is also altruistic, meaning it is purposefully used to the benefit of others.

An underlying theme of Stoicism is that you cannot be happy alone, you cannot achieve eudaemonia alone, you must do so with others, together as a family, a society, a civilization. You love others for *their* benefit, *their* sake, and if you get a dopamine fix because of it, then great! It ties into the importance of healthy relationships to achieve *eudaemonia*. Further, and probably most importantly, unconditional love requires acceptance and forgiveness. We are only human, after all, and we all make mistakes. To paraphrase the Bible, all have fallen short of the glory . . ..

For you to truly love without recourse, for you to rightly care for the happiness of others, for you to justly find your own sense of self-satisfaction, then you must strive to find ways to forgive your imperfections, your failures, and even your betrayals both in others and in yourself.

Easier said than done, I know.

An important caveat here is to explain what unconditional love *is not*. Love without expectation, forgiveness, and acceptance with grace is not an excuse to remain in unhealthy, toxic, or dangerous relationships. Conflict in relationships is normal and healthy to help resolve issues and grow in that relationship. However, living with narcissists, abusers, or those who are not providing a safe and nurturing environment is not normal. If you are in such a relationship, I would highly recommend putting this book down and seeking immediate help. As with anything in life where anything can be taken to the extreme, unconditional love can be used as an excuse to not escape an unhealthy environment.

TOO MUCH LOVE WILL KILL YOU

> "Shakespeare had it right all along: love will kill you in the end."
> —Raquel Capeda

Helen of Argos was said to be the most beautiful woman in the world. According to the Greek writer Homer, Helen's hand in marriage was won in physical combat. A pledge was made by all the losers that military aid would be provided to the winning suitor, in this story, King Menelaus of Sparta, should Helen ever be abducted from him.

A bit of foreshadowing, don't you think?

Thus, when Helen of Sparta met Prince Paris of Troy, her beauty overwhelmed him, and he whisked her away to become Helen of Troy. The mythos tends to agree that Helen went willingly either due to her unhappiness in her marriage to Menelaus or that her infatuation for and subsequent seduction by the younger Paris led her astray. Regardless, Menelaus called in the oath made by King Agamemnon to give him military support, and thus, the Trojan War and the first recorded war over love began. This is where it was penned that Helen had "the face that launched a thousand ships." In truth, if the Trojan War was more than a myth, Helen's abduction, or betrayal (depending upon which side of the battle line one is on), was a socio-political excuse for Mycenean Greece to launch a war of control of the Aegean Sea region but not the last war said to be fought for love.

Sticking with the mythical theme in Britain's Arthurian legend, Guinevere's betrayal of King Arthur with her affair with Sir Lancelot and the subsequent conflicts that followed, depending upon which epic you read, led to Arthur's death in battle and the destruction of Camelot.

In a more historically true epoch, Cleopatra VII of Egypt, the last of the Ptolemaic rulers of Egypt, had love affairs with senior Roman leaders Julius Caesar and Marc Antony, the latter of which committed suicide prior to her as the Roman Republic fell. Whether she truly loved either one is a matter of opinion among historians, but it romanticizes the idea of dying for love, much like in Shakespeare's various works on the theme.

In a metaphorical sense, love can kill a person by draining their emotional and mental reserves. It may be incredibly taxing to be in a relationship that is rife with drama and dissatisfaction. This kind of love can slowly sap our strength, hope, and joy. A person could feel as though their life is being sucked away, leaving them feeling hollow inside. Due to the body's persistent fight-or-flight response to the ongoing negative energy, it can also lead to physical stress. A person may eventually get so worn out by this kind of love that they experience total exhaustion, loneliness, and hopelessness.

What is really being discussed here is obsession. A person's obsession with someone can be an overwhelming feeling that dominates their life and thoughts. It may result in an unhealthy preoccupation with the other person, compulsive thoughts about them, and an attempt to manage their behavior. If there isn't any reciprocation, it might also result in envy and insecurity. Being conscious of your emotions is the first step in staying away from becoming overly fixated on someone. Consider why you are feeling this way and what steps you may take to make sure it doesn't happen again. It's crucial to keep in mind that being obsessed with someone is unhealthy for both parties and might have negative effects.

The next stage is to put your own needs first. Spend time engaging in activities that bring you delight, such as hobbies, physical activity, or just relaxing by yourself. Additionally, try to surround yourself with loved ones and friends who can support you emotionally. This can assist you in maintaining perspective and reminding yourself that life is about more than just being fixated on someone else. Additionally, if you notice that you are obsessively thinking about the person you are enamored with, take a break and engage in a fun activity to divert your attention. You can help yourself avoid falling too deeply in love by doing the actions listed below:

1. Try to keep your thoughts about the person to a minimum.
2. Refrain from romanticizing or idealizing the individual.
3. Avoid locations and activities that bring them to mind.
4. Refrain from communicating with them, even by text or email.
5. Discover new pastimes and pursuits to occupy your time.
6. Spend time with loved ones and friends who can support you.
7. Remind yourself that your obsession with this individual does not define who you are.
8. Talk to yourself kindly and constantly remind yourself of your value.
9. If necessary, get expert help.
10. Write out all the reasons you should not be fixated on this individual.

The only thing that truly matters in all of this is *how much* you love. When the last bugle blows, when life has come to its end, it doesn't matter what you looked like, how much money you had, how successful a career or business you had, the size of your house, how fast your car went, or even how much money was in your bank account. The only thing that will matter when you are laid in your casket or poured into your urn is how much you were loved. Your very purpose on Earth is to love. Love is a two-way street. To get it, we need to give it—but remember, unconditional love requires us to love without any expectation of receiving any of that love back.

AFTERWORD

> *A taste for irony has kept more hearts from breaking than a sense of humor, for it takes irony to appreciate the joke which is on oneself.*
>
> **—Jessamyn West**

If you can remember, I told you that the book was partially motivated by a friend telling me that I was hard to keep happy. It made sense. I needed a little bit of watering, like a cactus, but because I wasn't getting watered, I started to lean toward more humid conditions. I needed to uproot and find life's nectar to quench my thirst. I was inspired by her words. It made sense!

I was ecstatic to tell her that her words that I was hard to keep happy had moved me to write this book!

Except, that's not what she'd said . . .

What she *actually said* was that I was *not* hard to keep happy. What she meant by this was that I only needed a little watering and that, overall, I was content in life. It's easy to see how one could misread that, right? Maybe I heard what I heard because that's what I wanted to hear? After all, years spent around airplanes will sap your hearing. Regardless, it is moot because whether I am easy to keep happy or not doesn't mean both cannot be true. The two paradigms are not mutually exclusive. One can be both easy and hard to keep happy, depending on the circumstances. Holy hell! I almost feel like I must write another book just to help myself understand this concept!

Happiness is not a finish line after a long race. If it were, it would be worse because we would end up having to start over again and again on this journey to find prosperity and satisfaction. Here's the deal: we are told our entire lives that if we look a certain way, act a certain way, wear the right clothes, and say the right things, then we will be happy. If we are thin, attractive, stylish, trendy, and can "fit in," then we will be happy. The problem with all of that is that it's not true at all. Think of it: there are people out there who are the most beautiful people on the planet, and they are popping pills because they can't handle everyone looking at them. There are people killing themselves to stay up to date with the right clothing trends so they don't accidentally go out of style in the next five minutes. There are people who have millions of followers on social media and yet are suicidal because they feel so alone. The trick is that you have to stop caring what other people think about your weight, your hair, your shirt, your shoes, the way you talk, and the interests you have, or you will spend the rest of your days trying to please others who cannot even please themselves. That's no way to live and surely will not make you happy at all.

Everything in moderation. You don't have to be a gym rat, but don't be a couch potato. You don't have to be a billionaire, but living paycheck to paycheck isn't a great substitute. You don't have to have some storybook relationship, but being alone isn't amazing either. It is important to maintain proper balance in life. Like a beautifully made sword, one should be able to balance it on the tip of a finger. The weight will be felt, but it is manageable and awe-inspiring because each part is made in perfect harmony with the others.

Lastly, remember this is about your happiness. Do not be jealous of someone else's happiness. What makes them happy may not make you happy. What gives them joy may not give you joy. If you're chasing someone else's happiness, then you're simply losing out on your own.

Stay happy, my friends.

"You're going to realize it one day—that happiness was never about your job, or your degree, or being in a relationship. Happiness was never about following in the footsteps of all of those who came before you; it was never about being like the others. One day, you're going to see it—that happiness was always about the discovery, the hope, the listening to your heart and following it wherever it chose to go. Happiness was always about being kinder to yourself; it was always about embracing the person you were becoming. One day, you will understand. That happiness was always about learning how to live with yourself, that happiness was never in the hands of other people. It was always about you. It was always about you."

—Bianaca Sparacino

ACKNOWLEDGMENTS

I would like to take this opportunity to thank my wife and children for their ongoing love and support throughout my journey. Without their unwavering faith in me, I could never have written this book. Their love and encouragement are an invaluable source of strength and motivation. I am forever grateful for their unconditional love and understanding.

NOTES

All epigraphs from: *Brainy Quote*. (n.d.). Retrieved from https://www.brainyquote.com/

INTRODUCTION

Achor, S. (2010). *The Happiness Advantage: How a Positive Brain Fuels Success in Work and Life.* New York: Currency.

Kogan, N. (2018). *Happier Now: How to Stop Chasing Perfection and Embrace Everyday Moments (Even the Difficult Ones).* Boulder, CO: Sounds True.

Plato. (2007). *The Republic (Penguin Classics).* London: Penguin Classics.

VanNatta, M. (2019). *The Beginner's Guide to Stoicism: Tools for Emotional Resilience and Positivity.* Emeryville, CA: Althea Press.

CHAPTER 1: HAPPINESS REQUIRES HEALTH

Albers, S. (2010). The Twinkie Diet Being mindful of how much you eat matters. *Psychology Today.*

Ames, G., & Cunradi, C. (n.d.). *Alcohol Use and Preventing Alcohol-Related Problems Among Young Adults in the Military.* Retrieved from National Institute of Alcohol Abuse and Alcoholism: https://pubs.niaaa.nih.gov/publications/arh284/252-257.htm

Butler, B. a. (2021, June 29). *Military divorce rates compared to national averages.* Retrieved from Badonske and Butler Attorneys At Law: https://www.sadivorceattorney.com/blog/2021/06/military-divorce-rates-compared-to-national-averages/

Castaneda, R., & Fetters, K. A. (2021, May 4). *How Many Carbs Should You Eat to Lose Weight?* Retrieved from US News-Health:

https://health.usnews.com/wellness/food/articles/how-many-carbs-should-you-eat-to-lose-weight

CDC. (2021, March 22). *Adult Obesity Causes & Consequences.* Retrieved from Centers for Disease Control and Preventiom: https://www.cdc.gov/obesity/adult/causes.html

Disease Control and Preventiom: https://www.cdc.gov/obesity/adult/causes.html

Ericson, J. (2013, July 3). *75% of Americans May Suffer From Chronic Dehydration, According to Doctors.* Retrieved from Medical Daily: https://www.medicaldaily.com/75-americans-may-suffer-chronic-dehydration-according-doctors-247393

Fell, J. S. (2010, December 6). *A Twinkie diet? It comes down to calories.* Retrieved from Los Angeles Times: https://www.latimes.com/archives/la-xpm-2010-dec-06-la-he-fitness-twinkie-diet-20101206-story.html

Hosie, R. (2020, May 28). *You're probably not experiencing 'starvation mode' if your weight loss has stalled — here's what could be happening instead.* Retrieved from Insider.com: https://www.insider.com/truth-about-starvation-mode-and-weight-loss-2020-5

Kolata, G. (2016, May 2). *After 'The Biggest Loser,' Their Bodies Fought to Regain Weight.* Retrieved from New York Times: https://www.nytimes.com/2016/05/02/health/biggest-loser-weight-loss.html

Meerman, R. (2013, October 11). *The Mathmatics of Weight Loss- TED Talk.* Retrieved from Youtube.com

NAH. (2018, August 1). *A leading researcher explains the obesity epidemic.* Retrieved from Nutrition Action: https://www.nutritionaction.com/daily/diet-and-weight-loss/a-leading-researcher-explains-the-obesity-epidemic/

Pappas, S. (2010, Feburary 21). *'The Biggest Loser' Has Big Problems, Health Experts Say.* Retrieved from Live Science: https://www.

livescience.com/9820-biggest-loser-big-problems-health-experts.html

Pobiner, B. (2021). *Meat-Eating Among the Earliest Humans.* Retrieved from American Scientist: https://www.americanscientist.org/article/meat-eating-among-the-earliest-humans

Sapranaviciute-Zabazlajeva, L., Luksiene, D., Virviciute, D., Bobak, M., & Tamosiunas, A. (2017). Link between healthy lifestyle and psychological well-being in Lithuanian adults aged 45–72: a cross-sectional study. *BMJ Open*, 1-8.

The Truth about the Twinkie Diet. (2018, February 26). Retrieved from VCMBC: https://www.vcmbc.com/truth-twinkie-diet/

CHAPTER 2: HAPPINESS REQUIRES DISCIPLINE

CDC. (2021, March 22). *Adult Obesity Causes & Consequences.* Retrieved from Centers for Disease Control and Preventiom: https://www.cdc.gov/obesity/adult/causes.html

CDC. (2021, June 23). *Health and Economic Costs of Chronic Diseases.* Retrieved from Centers for Disease Control and Prevention: https://www.cdc.gov/chronicdisease/about/costs/index.htm

Fell, J. S. (2010, December 6). *A Twinkie diet? It comes down to calories.* Retrieved from Los Angeles Times: https://www.latimes.com/archives/la-xpm-2010-dec-06-la-he-fitness-twinkie-diet-20101206-story.html

Kolata, G. (2016, May 2). *After 'The Biggest Loser,' Their Bodies Fought to Regain Weight.* Retrieved from New York Times: https://www.nytimes.com/2016/05/02/health/biggest-loser-weight-loss.html

Krans, Brian. (2022). *Lawsuit: Coca-Cola Uses False Advertising to Sell Unhealthy Drinks.* April 7. Accessed May 27, 2022. https://www.healthline.com/health/coca-cola-false-advertising-unhealthy-drinks#soda-taxes.

Pappas, S. (2010, Feburary 21). *'The Biggest Loser' Has Big Problems, Health Experts Say.* Retrieved from Live Science: https://www.livescience.com/9820-biggest-loser-big-problems-health-experts.html

The Truth about the Twinkie Diet. (2018, February 26). Retrieved from VCMBC: https://www.vcmbc.com/truth-twinkie-diet/

CHAPTER 3: HAPPINESS REQUIRES LEARNING

Castaneda, R., & Fetters, K. A. (2021, May 4). *How Many Carbs Should You Eat to Lose Weight?* Retrieved from US News-Health: https://health.usnews.com/wellness/food/articles/how-many-carbs-should-you-eat-to-lose-weight

Ericson, J. (2013, July 3). *75% of Americans May Suffer From Chronic Dehydration, According to Doctors.* Retrieved from Medical Daily: https://www.medicaldaily.com/75-americans-may-suffer-chronic-dehydration-according-doctors-247393

Hall, K. (2009). Danny Cahill: What Happened? *Obesity Research & Clinical Practice (3) 3*, 207-210.

Low, J. (2020). Calorie Intake: How Many Calories Should I Eat? British Dietetic Association. Retrieved from https://www.bda.uk.com/foodfacts/calorieintake.pdf

Marks, G. A. (2019). Sleep problems in children and adolescents: A guide for practitioners. Oxford University Press.

Meerman, R. (2013, October 11). *The Mathmatics of Weight Loss-TED Talk.* Retrieved from Youtube.com

Spigt, M., Weerkamp, N., Troost, J., van Shayck, C., & Knottnerus, J. A. (2012). A randomized trial on the effects of regular water intake in patients with recurrent headaches. *Family Practice*, 370-375.

CHAPTER 4: HAPPINESS REQUIRES TEMPERANCE

Achor, S. (2010). *The Happiness Advantage: How a Positive Brain Fuels Success in Work and Life.* New York: Currency.

Altucher, J. (2014). *The Power of No: Because One Little Word Can Bring Health, Abundance, and Happiness.* Carlsbad, CA: Hay House, Inc.

Brown, B. (2015). *Daring Greatly.* New York: Avery.

Brown, B. (2018). *Dare to Lead.* New York: Random House.

Chua, R. M. (2019). Aquinas on Temperance. *New Blackfriars*, 5-21.

Geiger, B. B., & MacKerron, G. (2016, May 4). Can alcohol make you happy? A subjective well-being approach. *Social Science & Medicine,.*

Hoffman, H. (2012, April 25). *The Little Glutton.* Retrieved from PoemHunter.com: https://www.poemhunter.com/poem/the-little-glutton/

Hutchinson, D. (2016). *Lead with Balance: How to Work-Life Balance in an Imbalanced Culture.* Charleston: Advantage.

VanNatta, M. (2019). *The Beginner's Guide to Stoicism: Tools for Emotional Resilience and Positivity.* Emeryville, CA: Althea Press.

CHAPTER 5: HAPPINESS REQUIRES STRUGGLE

Case, S. (2020). *Hardcore Grief Recovery: An Honest Guide to Getting through Grief without the Condolences, Sympathy, and Other BS (F*ck Death; Healing Mental Health Journal for Adults After the Loss of a Loved One).* Naperville : SourceBooks.

De, A. (2022). *Over with Overthinking: Get rid of your overthinking in few easy, simple and everyday habits.* Kindle Books.

Estacio, E. V. (2018). *Imposter Syndrome Remedy: How to improve your self-worth, feel confident about yourself, and stop feeling like a fraud! (Psychology in your life Book 2).* PAME Code Publishing

Gagan, J. M. (2015). *Grow Up Your Ego: Ten Scientifically Validated Stages to Emotional and Spiritual Maturity.* Santa Fe: Rio Chama Publications.

Hehir, J. (Director). (2020). *The Last Dance* [docuseries].

Holiday, R. (2006). *Ego is the Enemy.* New York: Portfolio/Penguin.

Holiday, R., & Hanselman, S. (2016). *The Daily Stoic: 366 Meditations on Wisdom, Preserveance, and the Art of LIving.* New York: Penguin Random House, LLC.

Jenson, E. (2022, February 11). *'There is no relief': 'Dr. Phil' battles claims of toxic, racist environment in new report.* Retrieved from USAToday: https://www.usatoday.com/story/entertainment/tv/2022/02/11/dr-phil-phil-mcgraw-staffers-allege-toxic-racist-talk-show

Kübler-Ross, E., Kessler, D., & Shriver, M. (2014). *On Grief and Grieving: Finding the Meaning of Grief Through the Five Stages of Loss.* New York: Scribdner.

Mazique, B. (2012, January 11). *Michael Jordan's High School Coach Exposes Another MJ Myth.* Retrieved from bleacherreport.com: https://bleacherreport.com/articles/1020151-michael-jordans-high-school-coach-exposes-another-mj-myth#

VanNatta, M. (2019). *The Beginner's Guide to Stoicism: Tools for Emotional Resilience and Positivity.* Emeryville, CA: Althea Press.

CHAPTER 6: GROSS DOMESTIC PROSPERITY

Clason, G. (2014). *The Richest Man in Babylon.* Scotts Valley: Create Space Independent Publishing.

Cutler, H. C., & Dalai Lama XIV. (2009). *The Art of Happiness, 10th Anniversary Edition : A Handbook for Living.* New Yorl: Riverhead Books.

Dickler, J. (2022, November 16). *Credit card balances jump 15 percent, highest annual leap in over 20 years, as Americans fall deeper in debt.* Retrieved from CNBC: https://www.cnbc.com/2022/11/16/credit-card-balances-jump-15percent-as-americans-fall-deeper-in-debt.html

Gwartney, J. D., & Conners, J. (2009). The Crash of 2008: Causes and Lessons to Be Learned. *Social Education,* 63-67.

Graham, B. (n.d.). *The Intelligent Investor: A Book of Practical Counsel. Revised Edition.* HarperCollins e-books.

Kissell, C. (2022, October 18). *3 Simple Truths To Find Financial Happiness.* Retrieved from National Debt Relief: https://www.nationaldebtrelief.com/3-simple-truths-find-financial-happiness/

McElvaine, R. S. (1993). *The Great Depression: America 1929-1941.* New York: Three Rivers Press.

Milnas, D. (2022, October 18). *What Is the Average Credit Card Debt in America in 2022?* Retrieved from Moneygeek.com: https://www.moneygeek.com/credit-cards/analysis/average-credit-card-debt/

Okun, A. M. (1975). *Equality and Efficiency: The Big Tradeoff.* Washington DC: The Brookings Institute.

CHAPTER 7: RELATIONSHIPS AND HAPPINESS

Bradberry, T. (2015, October 21). *How Successful People Handle Toxic People.* Retrieved from Forbes.com: https://www.forbes.com/sites/travisbradberry/2014/10/21/how-successful-people-handle-toxic-people/

Bradt, G. (2015, May 27). *The Secret Of Happiness Revealed By Harvard Study.* Retrieved from Forbes: https://www.forbes.com/sites/georgebradt/2015/05/27/the-secret-of-happiness-revealed-by-harvard-study/

Canterbury. (2021). *Divorce Rates And Statistics In America.* Retrieved from Canterbury Law Group: https://canterburylawgroup.com/divorce-statistics-rates/

Cutler, H. C., & Dalai Lama XIV. (2009). *The Art of Happiness, 10th Anniversary Edition : A Handbook for Living.* New Yorl: Riverhead Books.

Gentry, W. D. (2008). *Happiness for Dummies.* Hoboken: John Wiley & Sons, Inc.

Gottman, J. M. (2015). *The Seven Principles for Making Marriage Work: A Practical Guide from the Country's Foremost Relationship Expert.* New York: Harmony.

Gottman, J. M. (2015). *The Seven Principles for Making Marriage Work: A Practical Guide from the Country's Foremost Relationship Expert.* New York: Harmony.

Harris, R. (2008). *The Happiness Trap.* London: Robinson Publishing.

Holt-Lunstad, J., Smith, T. B., Baker, M., Harris, T., & Stephenson, D. (2015). *Loneliness and Social Isolation as Risk Factors for Mortality: A Meta-Analytic Review.* Brigham Young University.

ISU. (2023). *René Spitz: The Effects of Emotional Deprivation.* Retrieved from Idaho State Univeristy :https://iastate.pressbooks.pub/parentingfamilydiversity/chapter/spitz/

Kogan, N. (2018). *Happier Now: How to Stop Chasing Perfection and Embrace Everyday Moments (Even the Difficult Ones).* Boulder, CO: Sounds True.

CHAPTER 8: PLEASURE AND HAPPINESS

Ames, G., & Cunradi, C. (n.d.). *Alcohol Use and Preventing Alcohol-Related Problems Among Young Adults in the Military.* Retrieved from National Institute of Alcohol Abuse and Alcoholism: https://pubs.niaaa.nih.gov/publications/arh284/252-257.htm

Aristotle. (2019). *Nicomachean Ethics.* Indianapolic/Cambridge: Hackett Publishing Compnay, Inc.

Cormier, Z. (2015). *Share to Facebook Share to Pinterest Share to Twitter ISBN: 0306823934 ISBN13: 9780306823930 Sex, Drugs, and Rock 'n' Roll : The Science of Hedonism and the Hedonism of Science.* New York: Hatchette Book Group.

Couples who have sex weekly are happiest More sex may not always make you happier, according to new research. (2015, November 18). Retrieved from Society for Personality and Social Psychology: https://www.sciencedaily.com/releases/2015/11/151118101718.htm

Destroyed My Brain.' Retrieved from ReleventMagazine.com: https://relevantmagazine.com/culture/billie-eilish-spoke-about-how-her-addiction-to-porn-really-destroyed-my-brain/

Geiger, B. B., & MacKerron, G. (2016, May 4). an alcohol make you happy? A subjective well-being approach. *Social Science & Medicine,*.

Harris, J. (2003). *Sex Is Not the Problem (Lust Is): Sexual Purity in a Lust-Saturated World.* Colorado Springs: Multnomah Books.

Holy Bible: New Century Version. (n.d.).

Johnson, B. (2022, February). *10 Reasons You Should Quit Watching Porn For Good.* Retrieved from DailyWire.com: dailywire.com/news/10-reasons-you-should-quit-watching-porn-for-good

Lampe, K. (2015). *The Birth of Hedonism: The Cyreniac Philosophers and Pleasure as a Way of Life*. Princeton: Princeton University Press.

Nisan, M. (1991). *The moral balance model: Theory and research extending our understanding of moral choice and deviation. In W. M. Kurtines & J. L. Gewirtz (Eds.), Handbook of moral behavior and development, Vol. 1. Theory; Vol. 2. Research; Vol.* Mahwah, NJ: Lawrence Erlbaum Associates, Inc.

Reid, R. C., & Gray, D. (2006). *Confronting Your Spouse's Pornography Problem*. Sandy: SilverLeaf Press.

Roberts, V. (2017). *The Porn Problem*. Charlotte: Good Book Company.

Sapranaviciute-Zabazlajeva, L., Luksiene, D., Virviciute, D., Bobak, M., & Tamosiunas, A. (2017). Link between healthy lifestyle and psychological well-being in Lithuanian adults aged 45–72: a cross-sectional study. *BMJ Open*, 1-8.

Schlossberg, N. K. (2011, November 1). *Happiness Is a Balancing Act: Happiness depends on the balance of positive to negative resources*. Retrieved from Psychology Today: https://www.psychologytoday.com/us/blog/transitions-through-life/201111/happiness-is-balancing-act

Stills, S. (2021, June 9). *Does more sex mean more happiness? Here's the science.* Retrieved from Women;s Health Network: https://www.womenshealthnetwork.com/sexual-health/does-more-sex-mean-more-happiness-heres-the-science/

CHAPTER 9: LOVE AND HAPPINESS

Bryant, J. D. (2016). *The Three Levels of Love*. KindleBooks.

Eggerichs, E., & Nelson, T. (2016). *Love and Respect: The Love She Most Desires; the Respect He Desperately Needs*. Nashville: Thomas Nelson.

Gottman, J. M. (2002). *The Relationship Cure: A 5 Step Guide to Strengthening Your Marriage, Family, and Friendships.* New York: Harmony.

Gottman, J. M. (2015). *The Seven Principles for Making Marriage Work: A Practical Guide from the Country's Foremost Relationship Expert.* New York: Harmony.

Holy Bible: New Century Version. (n.d.).

Keyes, K. (1990). *The Power of Unconditional Love: 21 Guidelines for Beginning, Improving and Changing Your Most Meaningful Relationships.* Love Line Books.

Manson, M. (2016). *The Subtle Art of Not Giving a F*uck. (A Counterintuitve Approach to Living a Good Life).* Harper KIndle Edition:HarperCollins Publishers.

Manson, M. (2019). *Everything is F*cked (A Book About Hope).* Harper Kindle Edition: Harper Collins Publishers.

www.ingramcontent.com/pod-product-compliance
Lightning Source LLC
LaVergne TN
LVHW041942070526
838199LV00051BA/2875